PENGU

THE GIFT OF

Katherine Schwarzenegger Pra_____, wife, daughter, sister, animal activist, and *New York Times* bestselling author. As a passionate animal advocate, Katherine works as an Ambassador for Best Friends Animal Society and the ASPCA, lending her time, voice, and energy to spread awareness about animal rescue. As an author, Katherine has skillfully translated her own personal experiences into all four of her books that speak to her generation. Katherine lives with her family in Los Angeles.

· · ·

Praise for *The Gift of Forgiveness*

"An inspirational book on learning how to forgive."
—*USA Today*

"Here's a sure conclusion from reading Pratt's book: The world would be a far better place if we practiced more of what the people Pratt profiles have discovered."   —Associated Press

"Affecting . . . Those looking for help with letting go and moving on will love [*The Gift of Forgiveness*]."
—*Publishers Weekly*

"Thoughtful . . . This contemplative book offers fresh insights with each immersion."   —*Booklist*

"Katherine is wise beyond her years. Everyone can learn a thing or two about forgiveness, especially now more than ever before."   —Jenna Bush Hager, cohost of *TODAY with Hoda & Jenna* and coauthor of *Everything Beautiful in Its Time*

"I believe this book will help many people to begin, participate in, and ultimately complete a cycle of forgiveness."
—Jamie Lee Curtis

"Katherine's book teaches us one of life's most important lessons: that through forgiveness we can find our own power."
—Gretchen Carlson, *New York Times* bestselling author of *Be Fierce*

"Katherine has written a smart, brave, personal book on something our society could use more of: the courage and grace of forgiveness. Everyone should read this."
—Rob Lowe

"I can't think of a topic that carries more life-altering promise than forgiveness, and this is just the book to guide us through."
—Kelly Corrigan, *New York Times* bestselling author of *The Middle Place* and *Tell Me More*

"Fascinating, moving, insightful, and immensely liberating. *The Gift of Forgiveness* will help you become strong at the broken places.
—Martha Beck, *New York Times* bestselling author of *The Way of Integrity*

"A powerful book that is astonishingly true, real, and uniquely universal. *The Gift of Forgiveness* shatters the barriers of the preconceived idea of what is or isn't an apology."
—Roma Downey, *New York Times* bestselling author of *Box of Butterflies*

"A great book to start a conversation and begin the process of healing. The stories within are illuminating, inspiring, and courageous."
—Bob Goff, *New York Times* bestselling author of *Dream Big*

"Katherine's book will enlighten, inspire, and ignite your own personal journey with forgiveness."

> —Judah Smith, pastor, founder of Churchome, and *New York Times* bestselling author of *Jesus Is ___*.

"A must read for anyone who has struggled with forgiveness in their life, and a necessary reminder for all of us that inner peace begins with self-love."

> —Mallika Chopra, author of *Living with Intent*

"Schwarzenegger Pratt tackles this tricky subject with compassion and empathy . . . and offers guidance on how to participate in the cycle of forgiveness." —*Parade*

"No matter your age or your belief system, there is something in this book for everyone. Read it and you will be inspired to reach for the gift of forgiveness."

> —don Miguel Ruiz, *New York Times* bestselling author of *The Four Agreements*

ALSO BY KATHERINE SCHWARZENEGGER PRATT

Rock What You've Got: Secrets to Loving Your Inner and Outer Beauty from Someone Who's Been There and Back

I Just Graduated . . . Now What?: Honest Answers from Those Who Have Been There

Maverick and Me

The Gift

of

Forgiveness

INSPIRING STORIES FROM
THOSE WHO HAVE OVERCOME
THE UNFORGIVABLE

Katherine Schwarzenegger Pratt

life

PENGUIN BOOKS
An imprint of Penguin Random House LLC
penguinrandomhouse.com
First published in the United States of America by Pamela Dorman Books
Life/Viking, an imprint of Penguin Random House LLC, 2020
Published in Penguin Books 2021

Copyright © 2020 by Katherine Schwarzenegger Pratt
Penguin supports copyright. Copyright fuels creativity, encourages diverse voices, promotes
free speech, and creates a vibrant culture. Thank you for buying an authorized edition of
this book and for complying with copyright laws by not reproducing, scanning,
or distributing any part of it in any form without permission. You are supporting
writers and allowing Penguin to continue to publish books for every reader.

Grateful acknowledgment is made for permission to reprint the following:
Page ix: Excerpted from *The Book of Awakening* © 2000 by Mark Nepo. Used with
permission from Red Wheel Weiser, LLC, Newburyport, MA,
www.redwheelweiser.com and Quercus Editions Limited, London.
Page 33: From *Your Best Life Now: 7 Steps to Living at Your Full
Potential* by Joel Osteen, copyright © 2004, 2007. Reprinted by permission
of Faith Words, an imprint of Hachette Book Group, Inc.
Pages 99 and 127: Reprinted by arrangement with The Heirs to the Estate of
Martin Luther King Jr., c/o Writers House as agent for the proprietor New York, NY.
Pages 169 and 179: Copyright © 2019 by Dr. Henry Cloud.

A Penguin Life Book

ISBN 9781984878274 (paperback)

THE LIBRARY OF CONGRESS HAS CATALOGED THE HARDCOVER EDITION AS FOLLOWS:
Names: Schwarzenegger Pratt, Katherine, author.
Title: The gift of forgiveness : inspiring stories from those who have
overcome the unforgivable / Katherine Schwarzenegger Pratt.
Description: New York : Pamela Dorman Life/Viking, 2020. |
Identifiers: LCCN 2019042526 (print) | LCCN 2019042527 (ebook) |
ISBN 9781984878250 (hardcover) | ISBN 9781984878267 (ebook)
Subjects: LCSH: Forgiveness.
Classification: LCC BF637.F67 S393 2020 (print) | LCC BF637.F67 (ebook) |
DDC 155.9/2—dc23
LC record available at https://lccn.loc.gov/2019042526
LC ebook record available at https://lccn.loc.gov/2019042527

Printed in the United States of America

Designed by Meighan Cavanaugh

Some names and identifying characteristics have been changed
to protect the privacy of the individuals involved.

This book is dedicated to my family and to all those who have practiced, or are brave enough to start practicing, forgiveness. It is dedicated to all those who have granted it, and received it as well. It is my hope that all of us come to realize that we are all struggling in some way, and that each of us can be a force of compassion, empathy, understanding, and love in another person's life.

"About Forgiveness"

The pain was necessary to know the truth
but we don't have to keep the pain alive
to keep the truth alive.

This is what has kept me from forgiveness: the feeling that all I've been through will evaporate if I don't relive it; that if those who have hurt me don't see what they've done, my suffering will have been for nothing. In this, the stone I throw in the lake knows more than I. Its ripples vanish.

What it really comes down to is the clearness of heart to stop defining who I am by those who have hurt me and to take up the risk to love myself, to validate my own existence, pain and all, from the center out.

As anyone who has been wronged can attest, in order to keep the fire for justice burning, we need to keep burning our wounds open as perpetual evidence. Living like this, it is impossible to heal. Living like this, we become our own version of Prometheus, having our innards eaten daily by some large bird of woundedness.

Forgiveness has deeper rewards than excusing someone for how they have hurt us. The deeper healing comes in the exchange of our resentments for inner freedom. At last, the wound, even if never acknowledged by the other person, can heal, and our life can continue.

—*Mark Nepo*

Contents

The Gift

of

Forgiveness

Introduction

I remember the exact moment when I knew I wanted to delve deep into forgiveness. I was standing in the parking lot of a local restaurant I love when, out of the blue, up walked the girl I'd once called my best friend.

We weren't just best friends—we were like sisters, inseparable since birth. We'd shared everything, from our birthdays to our clothes, our friends, our families, our secrets, and our dreams. We felt like we were one and the same; in fact, most people said our names together, viewing us as the pair that never split.

Then, more than twenty years into our friendship, we had a falling-out—one that shattered me down to my core. Her absence left a profound hole in my life. For the very first time, I was living without my best friend by my side, and I didn't know who I was without her. The end of our friendship affected all areas of my life. It was awful and it broke me.

After I was able to gain some distance and take time to process this change, I told myself I was okay and that I had forgiven the person I once thought of as blood. Shortly after declaring that I had moved on, though, I ran into my old friend and knew immediately that I was nowhere near over the end of our friendship. In fact, I wasn't even close to being over it. Standing in her presence, I felt anxious, scared, hurt, angry, and tremendously emotional, and I knew at that moment that I never wanted to feel like that again, especially around her.

It was then and there that I made a promise to myself: I would reengage in the work of forgiveness. This time I would go deeper. I decided to go to therapy weekly, and sometimes I even went twice a week. I sought help from my priest, my pastor, and I spoke to people of all faiths and no faiths. I talked to those of all ages, all backgrounds; I spoke to friends, and even to people I didn't know that well. I found that there were many who had similar experiences with unhealed ruptures. I went in search of stories of those who had forgiven so I could be inspired to forgive and move forward in my own life.

Some might think that having a fight with your best friend sounds trivial, but for me—and many others with whom I've spoken—it is not. I've come to learn that ruptures in relationships come in all shapes and sizes. And no one can tell you how to process a hurt like yours, what it will mean to you, or how it will affect your world.

I knew that, when it came to forgiveness, I had my work cut out for me—and if I didn't get this right, I would have that pit in my stomach for the rest of my life. I knew it would end up traumatizing me. The moment my old friend reappeared, I realized that forgiveness was a far deeper and more complicated subject than I had thought, and it was something I wanted to get better at practicing.

I am so grateful I decided to start the work of understanding forgiveness then, because it's truly the work of a lifetime. It's hard to get through life if you don't know how to forgive others, those you once loved and still love, and oftentimes, most challenging, how to forgive yourself. Forgiveness isn't about simply saying, "I forgive you"—it's about doing the work of *letting go*, which for me has proven to be the gift that keeps on giving.

When I look back on my journey of forgiveness, the most important thing I have learned is how powerful the gift truly is. I encourage everyone to try to welcome the gift of forgiveness into their lives. It is an endlessly fascinating journey that will allow you to continue to grow and be tested over time.

I am, of course, by no means an expert on forgiveness—in fact, I consider myself a student of forgiveness. I am constantly learning about the process, which is why I wanted to write this book and interview the people within about their unique journeys with forgiveness. The conversations we shared cover some of the most incredible accounts of inspiration, heartbreak, awe, and hope I have ever witnessed. But before I tell you how the relationship with my old friend ended up, let me take you back to the beginning, when I had my very first brush with "I'm sorry."

I WAS ON THE PLAYGROUND at school in kindergarten. I distinctly remember the anger in my five-year-old body when my friend lied to me about a playdate I had not been invited to. I remember going home and crying to my mom about how sad I was that my friend had lied to me. My mom explained that everyone makes mistakes and that we have to learn to forgive our friends. So that's exactly what I did. I went to school the next day and told my friend that I forgave her. She said she was sorry and we hugged and made up.

Years later, I came to learn that that was not, in fact, forgiveness. Forgiving too easily can lock you into unhealthy patterns that can last for years. By not properly addressing an issue or event, we avoid things we actually need to confront. We bury things that should, in fact, be unearthed, and we protect people who need to be given boundaries. I've learned that forgiveness can sometimes make you feel weak and other times can make you feel strong. It can trap you or it can set you free.

What I have come to learn is that real forgiveness is much more nuanced than what you learn in kindergarten on the playground. It's not a single step; it's not a simple "I'm sorry": forgiveness involves honesty, courage, self-reflection, the ability to listen closely. It involves the desire to forgive, and maybe not forget. And most importantly, it involves a lot of love, over and over again. Practicing forgiveness is its own reward, a gift both for yourself and for the world.

NOW, BACK TO MY OLD FRIEND. Today, I am happy to say we are friends. That pit in my stomach—and all the anxiety that once existed—is gone. Now we both have a lot of love and respect for each other, and we wish each other only the best. When we see each other, we laugh, share old stories from our past, and catch up on our present lives. This forgiveness is one that is *ours*; it is a shared journey, a choice we both made and continue to work on together. The goal was not to have the same closeness we had growing up; rather, it was about being able to make amends and move forward. I call this kind of forgiveness *conscious forgiveness*—a conscious choice we make and remake over the course of our lives to forgive and move on. Whether it's in your family, in your friendships, your marriage, separation, divorce, or even in death. It is a choice we make and continue to make forever.

The work I did on my own to understand the fallout from

the break in my friendship has also allowed me to take a deeper look at myself and at my own role in the friendship's demise. It also enabled me to look at other relationships, to see where I may have forgiven too easily, not communicated clearly enough, or buried resentments that came up in other ways. In learning how to forgive my friend, I also learned how to forgive myself, and others who I felt hurt by. All of this is what has pushed me to do my own brutally honest work, and to find a new way forward with love and forgiveness. I'm proud to say I have done so in all areas of my life. And all of that brings me back to kindergarten.

It turns out that the lesson I learned so many years ago on the playground had some truth to it after all. We are all human, we all make mistakes, and at some point in our lives we will all be in the position of either asking for forgiveness or granting it. The good news is that the power to ask for, or to give, forgiveness resides in us. So I urge you to move at your own pace, follow your heart, and embrace the journey.

I have struggled with forgiveness myself over the years in my own friendships, relationships, and family. I'm sure there will be moments in the future when I'll be challenged to forgive or ask for forgiveness again. That's why I'm so grateful to the people who shared their stories of forgiveness in this book. Each of them has walked a different path and lived a different story. What I take away from their journeys is personal to me, just as what you take away from reading them will be personal to you. That is why this book isn't about me. It's about the incredibly inspiring and moving people I interviewed, and it's about you. I wanted this book to speak to everyone—people of all ages, all backgrounds, and all faiths—because there is no right way or one way to forgive. There's only your way.

Each person I interviewed for this book has taught me that you have to stay the course, remind yourself that forgiveness is a process that comes with ups and downs, and never judge yourself or others along the way. My hope is that this book will make you feel less alone. I hope you will read it slowly, maybe one story at a time, think about it, and come back to it time and time again. That's what I did in writing it. Forgiveness done right is a gift, and, done well, it can work miracles.

What follows are stories of forgiveness—from names you may recognize, and others you won't. All can teach us valuable lessons. My hope is that you'll find inspiration within the pages of this book to help you on your own pathway to forgiveness.

Elizabeth Smart

Innocence Reclaimed

"Forgiveness is the answer to the child's dream of
a miracle by which what is broken is made whole
again, what is soiled is again made clean."

—*Dag Hammarskjöld*

In June 2002, when she was fourteen years old, Elizabeth
Smart was kidnapped from her bedroom in Salt Lake City,
Utah. She spent nine months in captivity, during which her
captors—a husband and wife—tied her up, raped her daily,
and threatened to kill her family if she made any attempts to
escape. In March 2003, she was rescued by police officers and
returned to her family. Such an ordeal would leave many of us
in a permanent state of rage, but, incredibly, not Elizabeth.
Shortly after her release, she made the decision to forgive her
captors for all the horrible things they had done to her—and
to move forward with her life.

Forgiveness did not come instantly; it was a process. Like

many, Elizabeth grew up with the idea that forgiveness was something simple, something she had learned on the playground: "When someone pushes you down, you're the bigger person when you say, 'It's okay. We can stay friends.'" When she returned home after being rescued, she still thought of forgiveness in this way. It took time for her to realize that forgiveness is not a gift you give to others; it's something you do for yourself—while also not excusing what happened to you. The horrible acts committed against her were in no way justifiable, but she discovered that she could accept her past in order to reclaim her future.

It wasn't until Elizabeth was trying to reacclimate to everyday life that she realized her childhood version of forgiveness no longer served her. She realized something crucial: "Forgiveness is not necessarily a two-way street. It's a very personal thing, and you don't need two people for forgiveness to happen." She learned that at the heart of forgiveness is compassion: compassion for the person who harmed you and, more importantly, compassion for yourself. As she told me, "It's loving myself. It's allowing myself to feel whatever emotions I feel and to deal with them. And if it's anger, you know what? I think that is just fine."

When Elizabeth first returned home, her mother told her that she should try her best not to relive her ordeal. Her captors had already taken so much from her; allowing them to maintain their grip on her by revisiting her captivity would be giving them too much control. She knew that staying angry at her captors wouldn't make any difference to them—it wouldn't punish them or erase any of the harm they had caused her. It would only trap her in her own cycle of trauma and rage. For her, holding on to this anger meant that she would never be fully happy: "I'd never be able to enjoy my life." Only once she recognized what was important to her—reclaiming her life— was she able to let go of that anger.

Despite all she went through, Elizabeth was still able to find reasons to be grateful. She pointed out that many kidnappings are committed by someone the victim knows. She told me, "I actually feel so lucky that I was kidnapped and abused by strangers, because most people who have experienced similar things know their captors. For me, I didn't have to have relationships with them. They were out of my life, so that made it much easier." Recognizing such glimmers of light, even in her darkest hours, has helped her on her journey forward.

While Elizabeth has chosen a path of forgiveness toward her captors, she admits that she still has moments when she struggles. She says it's normal for her anger or sadness to overwhelm her at times. "When you have those moments when you feel like you are falling back into anger or sadness," she told me, "allow yourself to feel those feelings, and then love yourself enough to let them go and to try to embrace your life moving forward." She advises people in similar situations to take their time. Working through these feelings is something that everyone must do at their own pace. Beating yourself up about still feeling those emotions only makes moving on even harder. Elizabeth suggests that recovery starts with acceptance: "Accepting that you're angry, accepting that you're hurt, accepting that something traumatic has happened to you. Then I would recommend doing your very best to start loving yourself. Don't even think about forgiveness at that moment. Just try to start loving yourself. I think as your love for yourself grows, you will be able to let go of what's happened to you."

To help strengthen her inner resolve, Elizabeth surrounds herself with supportive people—her friends and, above all, her family—who have helped her through her process of forgiveness and renewed her strength during her moments of backsliding. Setting goals for herself and relying on this network of positive people have helped her stay on track, especially when she experiences "emotional potholes" that might otherwise set her back. "I do everything I can to fill my life with the positive emotions, positive people, positive activities."

Surrounding herself with love also means distancing herself from people who might drag her backward. Her former captors have no role in her recovery. As she explains, "I didn't want to live my life under my captors' control, whether they were standing next to me or a hundred miles away locked up in prison. I did not want to live my life in fear, and I didn't want to feel like I had to be scared about everything and everyone." For Elizabeth, it was clear: dwelling on her captors would only hold her back, and she wasn't going to sacrifice her future for a past she could not change.

About a year after she had been rescued, Elizabeth was asked if she had forgiven her captors. She vividly remembers searching for an authentic response. "I felt like I had this sort of epiphany of what I felt true forgiveness was, and I remember feeling like, 'Yeah, I have moved on. I have let it go. I have forgiven.'" Her epiphany was that forgiveness is an act of self-love. Holding on to a traumatic past does nothing but consume your present emotional space. She has come to understand that "just loving yourself and giving yourself the freedom to live your life fully" is the key to moving on. Her understanding of forgiveness came "with growth and experience, and listening to other survivors, and going through a process of introspection that finally enabled me to articulate it."

Elizabeth's ability to move on was tested again when it was announced that her female captor, who was scheduled to get out of jail in 2024, would be released early, in September 2018. Although it was an incredibly stressful time, her forgiveness wasn't shaken; the self-love she worked so diligently to maintain over the years held firm. And the key to her remarkable strength is the love she has for herself. "I feel like I have a pretty good relationship with myself, and I'm proud of the person who I've become. I mean, I'm certainly not perfect . . . I definitely have plenty of flaws that I need to work on. But I like who I am."

When I first heard Elizabeth speak about forgiveness, I thought to myself, "How could she forgive two people who caused her so much pain and changed the course of her life?" But hearing how she was able to put aside the horrors she faced and instead focus on healing herself showed me that forgiveness starts, first and foremost, with *you*. Being kind to yourself, and allowing yourself to live the full life you deserve, is the first step to moving on. Elizabeth's journey through darkness teaches us all that forgiveness is truly an act of self-love.

Chris Williams

A Collision of Worlds

"That he that cannot forgive others breaks the
bridge over which he must pass himself, for every
man hath need to be forgiven."

—*Edward Herbert, 1st Baron Herbert of Cherbury*

On the evening of February 9, 2007, Chris Williams went
out for dessert with his wife and their three youngest
children. Within the hour, his life would be changed forever.
As he and his family drove back home, Chris recalls seeing a
car speeding down the hill, coming directly toward them. He
tried to swerve out of the way, but they were struck with tremendous force by the oncoming car. He recalls hearing the deaf-
ening sound of the impact. Once the car had come to a stop,
there was a deadly silence. As he looked over at his motionless
wife in the passenger seat, he knew she was gone. He struggled
to turn around to see if his children in the backseat were okay.
He looked at his son and daughter, both not moving, and knew

in that instant that they, too, were both gone. While he couldn't see his other son, he had a feeling that he was going to be okay. As he turned back to the front of the car, he looked at his lifeless wife, pregnant with their unborn child. He was numb with shock, unable to process what had just happened. He closed his eyes, feeling helpless and hopeless; the pain was unimaginable, and he wished he could die, too. Then he opened his eyes and saw the other car that had just hit him. He was suddenly overcome by a strange sense of peace. Despite the horror of the moment, he already knew that he would forgive the other driver.

While many of us would find it impossible to forgive someone who has taken so much from us, Chris knew that he had a choice to make. He recalls, "The one thing that nobody can take away is our ability to decide how we react to those situations. Was I going to go down the path that I knew wouldn't give me justice, wouldn't give me closure, wouldn't bring my family back? If anything, that path could actually poison the remaining family that I had with anger and vengeance. Or could I make a choice to let all of that go and choose to be healed in another way?"

Just as Chris had his own way of coping with the tragedy, so did the people around him. His mother had a very difficult time moving on from the sudden loss of her grandchildren and daughter-in-law. Right after the accident, he says his mother was unable to forgive. "She wanted vengeance. Whenever there was a parole hearing, she wanted me there, though I would never go." Chris's mother had to feel what it was like not to let it go. She learned that, for her, withholding forgiveness "starts to destroy you, it starts to eat you up. She finally realized, 'This is not for me, I can't do this.'" People often hold on to anger, thinking it will somehow heal their pain. Realizing that doing so just leaves them stuck in the midst of the trauma, unable to heal—that's when they turn to the only hope left for them: forgiveness. Being able to extend compassion despite suffering and loss has helped Chris cope with his pain. Holding on to anger is like keeping the wound fresh and open; you never give it the chance to heal.

Choosing the path of forgiveness gave Chris and his family peace. It also helped restore the life of the young man who had been driving the other car. His name was Cameron. For Chris, forgiveness was the only choice that would allow him to reclaim his life. He knew that seeking revenge would leave him locked in a never-ending cycle of anger and resentment. "Going down a path of anger or vengeance or desire for retribution—there's no happy ending down that path. It may make me feel good for a while, but it doesn't bring the people back. It doesn't make the pain and anguish go away. It just feeds into a poisoned atmosphere of anger and injustice."

Forgiveness wasn't easy. It was a constant struggle. As Chris describes it, "I found that this desire to let it go was like a battle, minute by minute. I'd say to myself, 'If I could do this for five more minutes, and then the next five . . .' Over time, it became a little easier to do. Gradually, I developed a greater ability to let it go. It's like an athlete getting better at the sport they're practicing." The ability to forgive gets easier as time goes by and you have a chance to develop what Chris calls "your forgiveness muscle."

Chris sees forgiveness not as an obligation, but as a gift: "I believe it's the greatest gift you can give yourself. It's your ability to regain control when you experience something that seems to take every choice away from you. It's an opportunity to feel relief when you might be in the most horrific pain. The person who forgives ultimately gets 100 percent of the benefit."

Forgiveness also helped restore the life of the driver of the other car. He says he always wanted what was best for Cameron, the young man who'd caused the accident. Amazingly, Cameron's health and well-being were always on Chris's mind, from the moment they were rushed into the emergency room. Chris remembers being in the ER and repeatedly asking about Cameron's status, even as he struggled with his own anguish. "Whenever I felt angry or sad, I didn't want to direct it at him, because that would bring him back into my life. What I wanted was the ability to go through those emotions, as powerful as they are, with my family and my friends and my loved ones." By channeling his grief away from its source and toward the support of his family and friends, Chris was able to let go of the trauma and deepen the bonds with the people he loved the most.

The secret to Chris's extraordinary ability to forgive lies in a burden that he has carried throughout his life—one that he knew Cameron would have to carry, too. When Chris was sixteen years old, he was driving to work one morning when he struck a young boy who had run out into the street. The boy was taken to the hospital. After clinging to life for several days, the boy died. Although there was nothing he could have done to prevent the accident, Chris has been tormented by the boy's death ever since. The boy's family was kind toward Chris after the accident, even writing him a letter attempting to relieve him of his guilt. Despite their understanding, Chris still suffered from the guilt of having taken a life. Decades later, when he lost his own family, he instantly felt empathy for Cameron. He knew that he and Cameron would now struggle beneath twin burdens: Chris would carry the grief of losing his wife and children, and Cameron would carry the guilt of having cut those lives short. But from the beginning, Chris found solace in empathy. Their shared burden became a bond between Chris and Cameron that helped each heal as they moved forward.

Chris didn't want the accident to consume Cameron's life; he wanted him to live a life of purpose. In one of their meetings, Cameron asked him, "After everything I did to your family, how can you forgive me?" Understanding the young man's pain and wanting him to move on, Chris asked Cameron to pick a date by which time he would have let it go.

Chris's forgiveness was inspired in part by his faith, something he could always fall back on when he needed reassurance. He knew that his wife and kids were in heaven, and he was guided by what he felt they would want for him. "My faith tradition is that they live on. In a sense, I felt like I was being watched. And I felt that they wanted me to be happy. If I got angry, my wife would suddenly appear and the first thing out of her mouth would be, 'What are you doing? Why are you sad? Why are you angry? We're okay. Move forward, and be happy. We'll all be together again.'" Thinking of his wife served as a constant reminder that choosing to forgive was the only way he could live.

Being able to trust in his faith allowed Chris to come to an understanding about the accident that had changed his life forever. Reflecting, he said, "Sometimes those tragedies, those trials that come into our lives, even if it's accidental—God has a way of taking that, and with his grace, making something amazing from it. Then it becomes the bedrock of a foundational experience in our lives that leads us on to greater heights."

For most of us, the process of forgiveness might seem impossible in the moment we need it most. Some of us may take months to get there, others years, and some may never be able to forgive. When I asked Chris if he had advice for people who felt like they might not be able to forgive, he said, "I would remind them to give yourself permission to grow. It's okay to give yourself permission to be on that journey forward. Don't expect to already be at the destination. Don't expect to immediately understand forgiveness." The same permission Chris gave himself helped him guide his own children in their struggle toward forgiveness. As he told me, "I think they really appreciated the fact that I was there for them throughout the journey, and it wasn't like I was expecting them to get to some destination immediately or expecting perfection." Everyone gets to forgiveness in their own way and in their own time. We need to be gentle with ourselves and kind to one another. Everyone will have moments when they need to feel supported—moments when they feel most alone.

Chris says that, for him, forgiveness is a practice. "It's really a way of living that says, 'I am going to retain control over my choices regardless of what others might do or say to me.' It is something you have to practice every single day so that you stay true to it." It is Chris's faith in the power of forgiveness that carried him through unimaginable tragedy, and restored his path to hope.

Chris's extraordinary story taught me a powerful lesson about forgiveness: the pain we carry from old wounds can open us to the pain of others. Our past mistakes can make us more empathetic, and old losses can make us more compassionate. Our struggles remind us of our humanity and make us capable of transcendent acts of kindness toward others, and ourselves.

Sarah Klein

Touched by Evil

> "Forgiveness has nothing whatsoever to do with how wrong someone else was; no matter how evil, cruel, narcissistic, or unrepentant they are. When you forgive a person, you break the ties with their ill deeds that keep you in anguish."
>
> —*Bryant McGill*

Sarah Klein grew up in a small suburb of Lansing, Michigan, known for its passion for the big state school Michigan State University. When Sarah was five years old, her neighbor invited her to a local gymnastics class. She immediately fell in love with the sport. Her mom signed her up for classes, and thanks to her natural ability, Sarah advanced quickly. Soon she was asked to audition for the competitive team. When she was just eight years old, a premed student named Larry Nassar joined her gym as a volunteer to get experience for his medical school application. For Sarah and the

rest of her teammates, Larry was seen as a safe and loving figure in the gym. This was in contrast to John Geddert, their
coach, whom Sarah describes as "an abusive narcissist who
would stop at nothing to win." Coach Geddert once shoved
Sarah's face in her own vomit after a strenuous practice while
verbally assaulting her. Next to the brutal tactics of Coach
Geddert, Sarah and her teammates saw Larry as "the nicest,
goofiest, most unassuming" presence in the gym, who "always
had a smile, was always friendly."

Larry set up his treatment room in an abandoned back
room in the gym and began treating Sarah for whatever injuries she suffered. He was very convincing, and because he
worked with the girls from a young age, his perverse treatments became normalized. He created a welcoming and caring
environment for his patients, so much so that Sarah recalls,
"We were always so happy to go back there because of what
John was doing to us in the gym. Larry was so nice and loving. He set himself up as a protector for us against John." He
played the role of the hero for the girls he was treating, so
when they were sent to him, they were relieved. They were
grateful for any chance to get away from their head coach.

During Sarah's time in competitive gymnastics, she saw
Larry for every ailment, and she became close to him. During
those ten years, she recalls "being vaginally and anally pene-
trated by him, three to four times a week, every week for my
entire childhood and into my adulthood." During his treat-

ments, he would only ever manipulate her body with his hands, but because his behavior had become so normalized, Sarah never realized that what she was experiencing was, in fact, sexual molestation—and deeply wrong. Sarah moved to New York City after high school and then to Minnesota for law school, and yet, every time she returned to Michigan, she would see Larry at the Michigan State University sports medicine clinic. After all, he was her friend and "the gym was family." His treatments were often full-body examinations. Sarah recalls that some of his treatments were legitimate, which made the sexual abuse that much more difficult to recognize. She says, "Larry really was doing a lot of what 'real' doctors do, too, which made it confusing. You spent more time at the gym than you did anywhere else in your life, and you went through these super high-pressure, high-stress situations together." Sarah had developed a bond with Larry, with whom she felt safe and cared for. He attended every doctor's appointment she ever had, and she even attended his wedding—that was the kind of closeness they felt for each other. But this closeness was a lie that hid his molestation.

It wasn't until her parents moved out of her hometown, when Sarah was twenty-five, that she saw Larry for the final time. She recalls feeling "like something in me just didn't feel right." She started working at a school and felt a lack of stimulation in her life. "I was just functioning less and less and less," she says. "And I became a shut-in. I would go to work and then come right home. I rarely socialized and had few functioning relationships." Sarah tried to make sense of it, but she couldn't. She remembers resigning herself to feeling that perhaps she was just one of those people who weren't supposed to be alive. She finally underwent therapy to find answers as to why she was feeling so lost—why she lived in a perpetual state of emotional pain, anxiety, and depression. There, she reflected on her time as a gymnast and the impact of the harsh, negative culture she was exposed to, but still nothing pointed to her experiences with Larry. "I would still—in those years of my twenties and early thirties—describe Larry as a great part of those memories for me."

It wasn't until Sarah was in her early thirties that her body began to shut down. She began feeling intensely painful pelvic cramps and became so sick, she was unable to keep food or liquids down. She was in and out of the emergency room, and no one was able to help her. Finally, she was diagnosed with a cyst on her ovary and told she had endometriosis. As Sarah began to research her diagnosis, she discovered the severity of her condition and its close link to infertility. This was particularly concerning as she had hopes of one day becoming a mother herself. She visited an expert in Atlanta who told her surgery was the next best step. When she woke up from the procedure, her doctor told her that in his twenty years of practice, he had never seen a case of endometriosis as severe as hers. He said, "Your bladder, your bowel, your ovaries, your rectum, your pelvic side wall, your ligaments . . . your whole pelvic anatomy was tethered together." Sarah ended up having to have her ovaries removed, able to keep only 10 percent of one ovary. After doing extensive research on endometriosis, she discovered that it was often linked to early childhood trauma, especially sex abuse.

After multiple pelvic surgeries, Sarah was able to get pregnant, and she now has a beautiful daughter. She says of her daughter, "When we talk about the forgiveness and the healing process, she's a big part of that for me."

When a 2016 article was published in the *IndyStar* featuring another former gymnast who'd come forward with sexual abuse charges against Nassar, Sarah was shocked. She says, "It was like getting hit by a train. I didn't even know what to do with it all. The realization that I had been abused for that many years by someone I absolutely loved was almost too much to handle." The enormity of abuse that she and the other girls had endured at the hands of Larry Nassar took Sarah a long time to process. Learning that her abuse "was the longest in duration and some of the most frequent in times per week" was even harder for her to fathom.

Having spent most of her life in the gymnastics world, Sarah knew that speaking out against members of the inner circle was highly discouraged. "The gymnastics world is like the mafia." She recalls once making a negative comment about her former coach and being heavily criticized by members of the gym and their parents, who couldn't see that she was being courageous for speaking out. Many girls felt that the harsh treatment they had received from their coach had ultimately contributed to their success as competitive gymnasts; they felt that "he did it because he loved us." It was, as Sarah says, a sort of "battered-woman syndrome."

Sarah attended Nassar's criminal sentencing hearing in January 2018, and said that "it was really empowering, but also really heartbreaking." She felt conflicted at the trial, seeing a man she had known so well and had loved so much, looking frail and old, having destroyed so many lives.

After Sarah read her statement, Larry's lawyer pulled her aside to tell her that it was "the most heartbreaking, strong, well-done victim-impact statement" that he had ever heard. When Sarah was reading her statement, Larry watched her the entire time, shook his head, and cried.

After the trial, Sarah was asked to do interviews about the sexual abuse she had suffered at the hands of Larry Nassar. Knowing how important it was to be a role model for her daughter, she agreed to do an interview as her redemption story. Afterward, she was asked by representatives from the Excellence in Sports Performance Yearly Award (the ESPYs) to accept the Arthur Ashe Courage Award on behalf of all the survivors who had been sexually abused by Larry.

Today, Sarah often gets asked, "How did you not know you were being sexually abused?" She responds, "Do people who are brainwashed in a cult see that brainwashing for what it is in that moment? Usually they don't. And then add to that being a child who has absolutely no point of reference for what is normal." Still, to this day, Sarah's healing process is ongoing. "I can appear put together, but it's still a process. A process that requires nurturing every day." Coming to terms with her abuse, and her compromised fertility, triggered rage in Sarah that still sometimes comes up.

It wasn't until after Sarah gave her statement in the courtroom to Larry, in front of everyone, that her process of forgiveness really began. "I think the forgiveness process did not start for me until after sentencing. Someone gave me the advice to walk my eight-year-old self up to that podium and speak for her—give her back the voice that had been taken from her. My heart was so broken, and it still is broken, for that little girl." She felt a shift occur in the courtroom that day. "I walked up there the troubled, scared, and fearful little girl. I walked away a grown woman. I got to take myself back, take my power back." Sarah realized that, by giving her statement, she was released from the burden of shame and rage that she had been carrying for so long. Forgiving Larry finally allowed Sarah to truly be present and active in her adult life.

Sarah's journey to forgiveness has also given her the opportunity to become a role model to women of all ages who have experienced similar abuse. She is a lawyer who solely represents other survivors of sexual abuse. Sarah wants other survivors, and her daughter, to look to her for guidance. She now understands that "we can actually help more people the more we can make peace with what happened. The freer of him I am, the more lives I can save and the more I can find peace in my own soul, in my own psyche." Sarah adds, "The more I forgive, the more I feel like I'm not in emotional prison anymore. Larry is the one in prison now. I forgive him, knowing that he's never going to harm me or anyone else for the rest of his life. Forgiving him gives me freedom to live up to my full potential as a woman, as an advocate, as a mom."

While Sarah has forgiven Larry, she has no desire to let him back into her life. "I think part of forgiveness is moving forward and being able to walk a little bit lighter into the next stage of your life. And if I was harboring rage and resentment and condemning Larry to the depths of hell, I couldn't be my best. So I let it go, and I made the very conscious distinction between forgiveness and reconciliation. Just because you forgive somebody doesn't mean you have to reconcile with them and let them back in your world. You can forgive them and still not be okay with them. And that distinction helps me forgive, too." Sarah says she has forgiven him for the abuse because "I have to, to be able to be free of him."

Reflecting on her journey, Sarah is thankful for the lessons she has learned and the wisdom she has gained. "I think that's part of the forgiveness process, too—coming to that place where I'm grateful that I got my struggles at the beginning of my life. Because now look what I can do. And I really am grateful for that."

Sarah's story offers hope to anyone who has been abused by someone they trusted. Nothing can erase the acts from the past, but it is our choice how we choose to move forward. She was able to get to a place where she could release her trauma, forging compassion from her suffering and strength from her vulnerability. Sarah's journey taught me that forgiveness doesn't always require reconciliation—that repairing the relationship isn't necessary, or may not be appropriate, for moving on with your life.

Polly Sheppard

Trusting in God's House

"When we don't forgive, we're not hurting the other person. We're not hurting the company that did us wrong. . . . We're only hurting ourselves."

—*Joel Osteen*

On the evening of June 17, 2015, Polly Sheppard attended her regularly scheduled Bible study group at Emanuel African Methodist Episcopal Church in Charleston, South Carolina. Toward the end of the session, her group rose for the benediction. As they all stood in prayer, eyes closed, a newcomer to their group that day, Dylann Roof, opened fire with a gun, taking the lives of nine church members. Polly's life was spared, but her close friends were not as lucky.

The shooting was senseless, motivated by a single, hateful fact: the shooter was white, and the victims were African American. Living through a mass shooting and losing close friends would leave most people filled with rage, but Polly

Sheppard reflects back on lessons from the Bible to help her move forward and live in a state of forgiveness. "The Bible says if you want forgiveness for yourself, you have to forgive others. Christ died on the cross for that forgiveness. He forgave the people who hung him on the cross. He said, 'Father, forgive them, for they know not what they do.'" For Polly, the overwhelming sadness of losing so many of her fellow church members was the greatest challenge. "You have to go through some stages to get to that forgiveness. I just know it comes to you, sometimes in the still of the night, when you're listening to that small voice who'll talk to you and lead you through what you're going through."

That "small voice" comes from her deep-rooted faith and her close relationship with God. Whenever Polly feels moments of sadness or times when her forgiveness is wavering, it's the soft voice of God that guides her forward. When she feels her faith being tested, she chooses to pray for others and for herself, asking for the wisdom to come out the other side stronger. For Polly, the stage of sadness in the immediate wake of the horrific event was her only time of unforgiveness. But when she saw a close friend coping with the loss of her son and embracing forgiveness, she realized that she, too, could move forward. Inspired by her friend's compassion, she understood that she needed to forgive Roof in order to heal.

Polly recognized that forgiving Dylann Roof was the key to her own salvation. But this realization wasn't immediate. It came to her after "sitting here with all this unforgiveness in me toward him. Who am I hurting? I'm just hurting myself." She knew that Roof had no remorse and didn't dwell on the horrible actions he had committed. Roof was able to move forward, unburdened by his crime, while Polly was holding on to sadness, frozen in grief. If she nurtured her grief, she knew that she would only be hurting herself. So she relied upon the lessons learned growing up in a large churchgoing family, lessons that guided her inevitably toward an embrace of forgiveness. Polly was confident that her faith in God would allow her to overcome any and all challenges that lay before her.

As Polly told me, there were times in her past when she did not forgive so quickly, times when she held on to anger. She sees this reluctance to release anger as a natural part of the process of healing: "Forgiveness comes to us in stages, and feeling that forgiveness is impossible is one of those stages." Keeping the anger alive can be a person's way of coping in the early stages. But when you allow yourself to talk about the situation, you may discover that forgiving is the better option.

Polly recalls once having a conversation with an older Jewish man who told her that he was unable to get along with his children. He complained that his children were all disappointments—none of them liked to work—and then he began to rail against Hitler for his unforgivable acts. Polly could see the man was locked in a cycle of bitterness, so she told him, "Well, Hitler is dead. Worms have eaten his body by now. Are you gonna go around letting this dead man control your freedom and thoughts? Eventually, you have to forgive him." The man was startled by Polly's frank response, seeing for the first time how the tragic events of long ago had shaped his thinking. The man told her that he was going to call his children and forgive them. As for Hitler, however, he wasn't able to forgive. When it comes to forgiveness, Polly said, "We come to it in different stages. Everybody doesn't forgive the same way, and some people may never forgive. That's just their way of coping."

For Polly, forgiving Dylann Roof took about three weeks. She doesn't look at him with anger in her heart the way most might think she does. She says, "I just think he's a lost soul. Sometimes I wish I could talk to him and see what's actually in his mind. He said why he was doing it, but I just wish I could sit down and talk to him." She remembers hearing that when Dylann was interviewed by the FBI, he told them he'd almost abandoned his murderous plot because of how kind the church members were to him. Polly remembers, "When he got to me, he told me to shut up and that he wasn't going to shoot me. He was gonna leave me to tell his story." She used to wonder why she was spared while so many others were killed. During the court hearings, Polly finally got her answer. Dylann told the court, "She was looking at me, so I couldn't shoot her."

Today, Polly lives her life free of the burden of bitterness, and thinks of Roof with empathy and compassion. "I felt sorry for the young man, 'cause he's twenty-one and he's a lost soul. He needs to accept Christ and repent for what he's done. And if God forgives him, he's good. Actually, he'll make it to the other side." Polly believes that, given the opportunity, she could help Dylann recognize their common humanity. As she says, "If I sat across the table from him, I could help him think a different way." She hopes that he would be able to listen to her, and she hopes that one day he might be able to say that he is sorry for the lives he took in that church. Speaking of her choice to follow the path of forgiveness, Polly notes, "You think you're letting someone else off the hook, but you're letting yourself off the hook. Because if you don't have that forgiveness, you're not gonna heal."

That day, Polly lost close friends—friends who felt like family. She could have fallen into bitterness, but instead she looked to her faith to understand Dylann Roof. Many of us who grew up in houses of worship learn about the importance of forgiveness, but this doesn't guarantee we'll be able to abandon hatred, especially after such a horrific incident. But Polly's faith is deep and firm, and it allowed her to have compassion for the shooter, despite all that he took from her.

Polly's story shows the power of compassion, even in the face of blind hatred. She could have matched hate for hate and carried her bitterness to the end. No one would have blamed her. Instead, her heart has remained open. I was particularly moved when Polly said that she wished she could talk with Dylann. Even after everything he had done, that she would still want to have a conversation with him showed me that looking past the unimaginable—perhaps even unforgivable—actions of an individual to lend a helping hand or a listening ear can make all the difference in the world to someone in pain. Though Polly wasn't in a position to do so before the tragedy at the Emanuel African Methodist Episcopal Church that day, living each day with an open heart and compassion for others is what's important, whether we find the strength to do so through our faith or by some other means.

Christy Little Jones

Regaining Trust When
Vows Are Tested

"There is no self-love without forgiveness, and there is no forgiveness without self-love."

—*Bryant McGill*

Christy Little Jones always knew that marriage and family would be the center of her life. As a girl, she would fantasize about her future husband and the excitement around being his wife. Years later, her dream would be tested, and it would prove to be more challenging than she could have ever anticipated.

When Christy first met Adrian, he "literally swept me off my feet." She fell hard for Adrian, and "felt protected and safe, like he's got a plan for our life, for our family and marriage." It was like nothing Christy had ever experienced before; she knew they would spend the rest of their lives together. Their fairy-tale life had begun; they were madly in love. They got married and had three babies in just a few years.

In 2005, Christy and Adrian started a marriage ministry at their church. As a couple, they would take other couples through premarital classes—classes to introduce them to the process of engagement and to prepare them for what was to come in marriage. Christy and Adrian also helped couples work to make sure their unions stayed strong. She says, "It really was my purpose in life to be a champion for marriages, and for families, and for the togetherness that I really believe marriage is designed to be." They were the picture-perfect couple, and they were helping so many others work through their rough patches to come out the other end with their marriages still intact.

Christy and Adrian's counseling classes and their own relationship seemed to be going well, until the day that Christy received an email from one of her blog followers. The email came from a young woman who knew the passion Christy had for her own relationship and the relationships of everyone around her. In her email, the woman detailed her recent experience on a flight with Adrian, who was traveling with another woman and showering her with affection throughout the trip. The woman told her that she knew how much of a champion Christy was for the institution of marriage and how much she believed in love, so it pained her to write the email, but she had to. Christy called Adrian and asked him about the email.

He quickly denied the accusations, but she noticed a change in his demeanor. Still, she decided to let it go. A few weeks later, Christy received an email from another stranger that said, "Hi, Christy. I know you don't know who I am, but I am no longer dating your husband."

Christy's greatest nightmare had come true. She reread the email, then sat down at her desk and called Adrian. He denied knowing the woman, became defensive and angry, then hung up. Moments later, a sobbing Adrian called Christy back and admitted he had had an affair. He told her he realized it had gone too far after the woman admitted she had fallen in love with him, and he quickly ended their relationship.

Christy called her pastor and asked for help. When she sat down with him, she said it was like facing a disappointed father; her pastor was deeply invested in the success of her marriage and was pained by Adrian's infidelity. Christy knew she wanted to surround her marriage with people who would "support us and protect us during this time of healing." She and her husband began their healing process alongside their pastor and focused on talking things through. When they returned home from their first meeting, Christy did the unimaginable. "I literally told him that I forgave him, and when I said that, he fell down and broke down and was like a heap bawling, crying on the ground."

Having been a product of divorced parents, and knowing the devastation that it had caused, Christy knew that that was not the route she wanted to take in her own marriage. It was not the legacy she intended to leave for her children. Christy believed that the pain of divorce "can be generational if you don't stop it." Although divorce might have been the easier route, it was important to Christy that she and her husband try to make their marriage work. They were both on the same page: they wanted to fight for their relationship, and so they fought together. She wanted her husband to know: "I love you. I'm in this. Let's fight for this." Christy also said, "I'm a woman of strong faith, and so I believed that God was going to heal my marriage."

A few days after finding out about her husband's affair, Christy got an email from a couple asking about marriage coaching. She felt she needed to focus on her own marriage, so she told the couple she could refer them to someone else for the time being. The couple informed her that they had seen a picture of Adrian on a cheaters site, listed as "cheater of the week," and followed it up with a link. In the following hours, her inbox began filling up with emails from women sending her their concern because they, too, had seen her husband on the site. Christy visited the site and saw that the image of her husband had already reached 180,000 views and counting. Eventually, the image was removed.

Despite the public exposure, Christy remained true to the process of healing that had begun the moment she told her husband she had forgiven him. Seeing Adrian break down showed

Christy that "when people do something like this, it breaks them, too. It's not only the victim who is broken or hurt; the person who commits the adultery is broken, too." Adrian was carrying the guilt not only for what he had done to his wife, but also to his family. He would say, "I can't even look at myself in the mirror." Christy knew her husband needed her love and support to get through the process, and she needed his.

Throughout Christy's journey, Adrian was there for her as she worked on forgiving him. When they would have challenging days, days when Christy wanted to ask Adrian about his affair, he would answer her, no matter how many times she asked the same question. She had times "where I would go through anger and I wanted to break every bone in his face. I wanted to have the satisfaction of hurting him as much as he hurt me." She would voice those feelings and emotions to her husband, and he would listen and accept her anger.

Through her coaching, Christy had experience with marriages undergoing hardship. She has come to recognize five stages of reconciliation: first shock, followed by anger, then sorrow, then acceptance, and finally forgiveness and healing. "You've got to get out of the cycle, and the only way to get out of the cycle is by forgiving. And most people don't know how to forgive." By truly forgiving someone, you are giving a gift, completely and without reservation. Christy says to imagine the gift of forgiveness as a big present wrapped with pretty bows. Some people present the gift but can't let it go—leaving them trapped in resentment. When you are able to hand over that beautiful gift and release it—not expecting anything in return—*that* is when you have really given the gift of forgiveness.

As Christy struggled to release her anger, Adrian underwent his own journey. For him, the process involved recognizing what was most important to him. As Christy says, "It was a hard issue for him, and he had to work through it in order to recognize the value of his marriage and the value of his family." The process had its ups and downs. "We cried when it was hard. We prayed when it was hard. We celebrated when it was an easy day, and we stayed very connected and close. It really felt like the weight of the infidelity lifted at about twelve weeks."

After three months of soul-searching, Christy felt she had finally reached forgiveness. She and Adrian could start a new chapter in their lives, coming together to rebuild the trust that had been broken. Working through the struggle of her husband's infidelity came with a shift in both the intimacy and communication of their marriage. In the beginning, Christy saw herself as the victim; but through the process of forgiving, she discovered a wealth of empathy and compassion for Adrian as he struggled to forgive himself. "Something that was so painful and so difficult for both of us really was a blessing, because it helped us to become more emotionally connected with each other. What was beautiful about it was I do believe that everything happens for a reason." It wasn't easy, but she is at peace knowing that she listened to her heart, fought to re-build her marriage, and finally arrived at a place of love, trust, and commitment. At the end of their healing and rebuilding process, Adrian and Christy decided to rededicate themselves to each other and to their marriage. Today, they are happier than they have ever been.

Christy's story moved me deeply. At first, I was sur-prised by how quickly she was able to tell her husband that she forgave him. After speaking with her, I believe that, by telling Adrian he was forgiven, Christy was setting her intention; full forgiveness took years. Hear-ing how much she cared for her husband during their healing process forced me to look at betrayal in a differ-ent way. When the person who strays is truly sorry, they suffer as well, and it can be even harder for them to for-give themselves than it is for their partner to release blame. Every betrayal is unique, and our reactions are our own. But Christy's choice shows us that—with a com-mitted partner—forgiving can be a way to strengthen a relationship that might otherwise be abandoned.

Immaculée Ilibagiza

Healing the Wounds of War

> "Nothing is more generous and loving than the
> willingness to embrace grief in order to forgive."
>
> —*Brené Brown*

On April 6, 1994, an airplane carrying Rwanda's president, Juvénal Habyarimana, was shot down, sparking widespread violence across the country between its two main ethnic groups: the majority Hutus and the minority Tutsis. Within hours, a slaughter of the Tutsis, which had been organized prior to the president's assassination, began, leading to the mass murder of more than one million Rwandans—primarily Tutsis— over the span of just one hundred days.

Tensions between the two ethnic groups had been simmering for decades, exacerbated by policies put in place by the Belgians during their colonial rule. With the death of President Habyarimana, an elite group of Hutu extremists declared their intention to kill all who belonged to the Tutsi tribe. Almost instantly, the Rwandan Patriotic Front (RPF), a Tutsi-backed rebel army, entered the country from neighboring Uganda to come to the aid of their fellow tribespeople. Within three months, the RPF had succeeded in driving the Hutu-dominated government into exile, along with the most egregious perpetrators of the genocide. Yet many Hutus remained in the country.

As the killing spree came to an end, the country was in a state of massive devastation. The government was left with a terrible legacy; so many people had participated in the killing that it would be impossible to prosecute them all.

In July 1994, a new government was sworn in. Pasteur Bizimungu, a moderate Hutu, became the country's new president, and Paul Kagame, a Tutsi and former commander of the RPF, became vice president and minister of defense. In 2000, Kagame was elected president.

The government was left with the task of bringing justice to the victims of this terrible crime. The leaders of the genocide were driven off, imprisoned, or killed. But for the tens of thousands of Hutus who had cooperated—either willingly or through coercion—incarceration was impossible. So Kagame asked the Rwandan people to do the one thing that could reunite their fractured country: he asked them to forgive.

Given the scale of the murder and the devastation that the Tutsis had endured, it seemed almost cruel to ask them to forgive, but Kagame did just that. He saw that the only way for the country to move forward together in unity was to forgive and start anew. In every town and village across the country, meetings were organized. In these meetings, villagers would sit down and hear from both the victims and the attackers. The victims who managed to survive could talk about what they had experienced and about the loss of their family and friends, while the people who had participated in the killings would listen and then plead for forgiveness. While not everyone agreed with this method of moving the country forward, most people complied.

Immaculée Ilibagiza was one of the survivors—one of those countless victims called upon to forgive crimes most of us could never fathom. When the Rwandan genocide started, Immaculée was home on a break from school. Her brother woke her up with the news of the death of the president. She remembers hearing the chaotic reports on the radio and feeling a sense that something catastrophic was about to happen.

That morning, Immaculée remembers her father giving her a rosary and instructing her to go to the house of her neighbors, a Hutu pastor, for safety. As she left her family behind, she had a premonition that she would never see them again. Her father was loved by many, and he always told her not to judge others. It was because of his selfless demand that she flee that Immaculée is alive today. She remembers getting to her neighbors' home and being instructed to hide in the bathroom. Unable to speak or cry, she would remain in that bathroom for the next ninety days.

As she sat in the bathroom with seven other women, she would listen to the radio and hear about the killings occurring outside those four walls. Immaculée remembers those first few days in hiding—her sense of hopelessness, losing all faith that she would ever get out alive. "I felt so much anger, I couldn't even pray," she recalls. It was then that she heard a group of Hutu men inside the home, searching for any Tutsis who might be hiding. She remembers in that moment begging God to restore her faith in Him. As she heard the men outside the bathroom door, she knew it was only a matter of time before they found her and the other women, and they would all be killed. She closed her eyes and said, "Please, God—not today." Then she said: "If there is a God and the presence of Him is real, please don't kill me today." For some time leading up to that moment, she had doubted that God even existed, but that day she prayed and wanted so badly to believe. The men searched the whole house, and when they came to the bathroom door, they stopped, turned to the owner of the house, and told him that they trusted him. Their search ended and they left the house. From this moment on, Immaculée's faith in God was restored.

While she sat in the bathroom, she thought about the feelings of the women beside her, and about those of the people committing murder. She thought of her family, whose lives she feared had been taken. She felt anger and hate—hate for being stuck in that bathroom, for the state of Rwanda, and for the loss endured by so many. She spent bitter months trying to convince God that she had a right to be angry, a right to feel rage. She began to pray and speak to God, in an open and honest way. She felt anger for the loss of her family. Looking back, she now sees that "anger is like an obstacle."

At that time, Immaculée made plans for what she was going to do to seek revenge once she got out of hiding; most of these plans involved acts of violence for the deep anger she was feeling. While imagining the violence she would inflict upon the killers, she suddenly realized that this sort of hatred was, in fact, the very source of the horror that had consumed her country. She quickly realized that "anger and hatred become a sickness," and holding on to those feelings would only make her sicker—it wouldn't do anything to help her feel better. "It is why God made us as a family. What hurts one, hurts another."

While Immaculée was in hiding, she diligently read the Bible and discovered that it called on believers to "love one another, pray for those who hurt you, and love your enemies." She would say her rosary daily, but when she would recite the Lord's Prayer, she would get caught on the line "Forgive us our trespasses, as we forgive those who trespass against us." As she recited the prayer, she knew she didn't believe it. She kept saying to herself, "If I forgive them, that means they're right and I'm wrong." It was then that she asked for help from God. She prayed to God, saying, "Help me to forgive." She said, "Forgive them, Father, for they don't know what they do." It was only then that she felt a huge weight lifted off her shoulders. Finally, she felt she could forgive. Immaculée says it was her strong belief in God and feeling His presence that allowed her to forgive.

Finally, after ninety-one days in hiding, the murders ceased. Immaculée stepped out into the world with a sense of peace and happiness—happiness to be free once again, and peace for the work she had done while in hiding to begin to forgive and be free of hate. But she now indeed faced a life without her family, and that pain is something that may never leave her.

Throughout her process of forgiveness, Immaculée drew inspiration from the people she most looked up to, people like Gandhi, Martin Luther King Jr., and Mother Teresa. "These were the people whom I admired, and no matter how much they suffered, they always did what was right." She made the decision to live a life without bitterness—emulating the great heroes of peace and forgiving those who had killed her family.

Eventually, Immaculée decided to go to the jail to see the man who had killed most of her family, wanting to make sure that she had actually done the work to truly forgive. When she confronted him, she realized that he didn't know what he had done. She broke down and "cried out of compassion for him." She asked him, "How can you welcome such evil?" She then told him, "I forgive you." She explains that she saw him as a blind man who didn't know what he had done, and "all I wanted to do was give him God."

This was a man she had known and respected like a father, and yet he was the one who had killed her family—all because they belonged to different ethnic groups. She remembers crying and breaking down in front of him. While she sat with him, she felt that "even in my sadness, there was serenity and comfort deep down." She realized she never wanted him to experience any kind of pain. It was then that she knew she really had done the work to forgive him.

Whenever Immaculée feels anger—for the things she lost in the genocide, or any other injustice—she asks God for help. She tries to be patient with herself. She reminds herself that "there is always someone in a worse situation," which allows her to keep things in perspective. When people say they are struggling with forgiveness and learning how to forgive, she tells them what forgiveness feels like: it feels like peace. "If I hurt another person, it won't bring back my mom or my brothers or my father," she says, acknowledging her ability to forgive someone who took so much from her. Knowing her anger wouldn't fix what had already happened and wouldn't bring back what she'd lost, Immaculée understood the only way she could move forward and live a healthy life was to forgive.

Years later, Immaculée recalls talking about her past with someone who said to her, "You are not damaged. What you are missing is the affection of your parents, and that is understandable. There is a way you can fix that." She didn't understand how she could possibly fill the void of not having the affection of her parents. The man told her, "Love those who need to be loved most"—and that would be how she could get back the feeling of her parents' affection. She began volunteering at orphanages and helping those in need. Doing this helped to fill the space in her heart. By giving love, love comes back to you. That is how Immaculée chooses to live her life.

When I heard Immaculée speak about how big a role love has played in her healing process, it made me think of how I could implement that into my own journey with forgiveness. We tend to jump immediately to hate or other negative emotions when someone has wronged us, even if it involves people we love deeply. Now, when I am hurt by someone I care for, I try to heal myself by sending them love instead of anger. I hope that doing so helps them get to a place where they can heal in their own way, too. But I keep in mind that the very act of sharing loving energy with them will come back to me in a healing way. I think it's so important to see forgiveness as a healing process—one that promotes loving ourselves as much as loving others.

Ron Hall

Working Our Way Home

"They who forgive most shall be most forgiven."
—*Philip James Bailey*

When Ron Hall decided to admit to Debbie, his wife of many years, that he had had an affair with another woman, he was not prepared for her response. "I had an affair, and she forgave me for it. She said, 'If you will never do this again, I will never mention this again. We will wipe the slate clean, and you will be forgiven.'" Experiencing Christlike forgiveness was something that Ron had heard about several times, but it wasn't until he experienced it firsthand that he knew it was real. His wife had granted him the kind of forgiveness that most people dream of receiving. She said to him, "You're not going to live under this condemnation. You are forgiven, and we'll build our lives back together." In return, he told her he would do anything she asked of him for the rest of their lives together. In response, his wife said, "I just want you to be a faithful husband. That's really all I expect." From then on, Debbie never brought up Ron's affair again.

It wasn't until ten years after the affair that Debbie asked Ron to do something that pushed him outside of his comfort zone. Debbie had had a dream from God about a homeless man, in which God asked her to befriend the homeless man. Determined to find him, Debbie told Ron about her dream and asked him to help her fulfill God's mission for her. Ron initially thought her dream seemed a little bizarre, but he had promised her to do whatever she asked of him. The next morning, they drove to the inner city of Fort Worth, Texas, searching for the man from Debbie's dream. They drove down backstreets and alleys, and after driving around for hours, they decided to stop and volunteer at a homeless shelter. They had been serving in the shelter for about two weeks when a shirtless man stormed in, screaming at the top of his lungs that he was going to kill whoever had stolen his shoes. The man began throwing tables across the room and hitting people. While Ron got to his knees to hide, Debbie jumped up and down, shouting, "That's him, that's him! That's the man in my dream!" Ron was stunned. Debbie looked at him calmly and said, "Ron, I believe I heard from God that you have to be his friend."

Ron wasn't exactly eager, but he knew what he needed to do. In the following weeks, he asked around for information about the homeless man. The man's name was Denver, but most people called him Lion of the Jungle because he ruled the streets with fear and intimidation. Others called him Suicide, "because messing with him was equivalent to committing suicide."

Over the next five months, Ron drove to the inner city, passing by Denver every day. Ron tried to convince him to get in his car so he could befriend him as his wife had asked. One morning, to his horror, Denver accepted. Ron could sense the anger seething within his passenger. Denver asked Ron why he had been bothering him for so long. Ron replied, "Man, I just want to be your friend." Denver responded in a low growl, "Man, I might think about that." It was clear that Denver wasn't looking to add any friends to his list, but Ron was persistent. He had no clue why Denver wouldn't want to become friends with him; Ron was well-off and could provide clothing, food, and help for someone in his position.

A few weeks later, Ron saw Denver again, out on the streets searching through a dumpster, and asked him to join him for some coffee. Denver told Ron to leave him alone. Ron replied, "I would, but my wife says we have to be friends." So Denver agreed to go get a coffee, but only after making one thing very clear to Ron.

"Well, I heard when white folks go fishing," said Denver, "they do this thing called catch and release. I don't get it. Because back on the plantation where I grew up in Louisiana, we'd go out in the morning and dig us a can full of worms, get us a cane fishing pole, and sit on the riverbank all day. And when we finally got something on our line, we were really proud of what we caught. So it occurred to me, if you just a white man fishing for a friend, and you gonna catch and release, I ain't got no desire to be your friend." It was then that Ron realized Denver's wisdom. Ron was instantly hooked, and he decided to enroll in the "school of Denver." Ron would drive down to the inner city every day and sit on the curb with Denver, listening to what he had to say. While getting to know each other, Ron learned that part of Denver's hesitation with befriending Ron and Debbie had to do with his upbringing on the plantation. As a fifteen-year-old, he was roped and dragged by the Ku Klux Klan for helping a white woman change a flat tire. The Klan made Denver promise that he would never speak to or approach another white woman again, and it wasn't until meeting Debbie that he had disobeyed the Klan's orders. Later, Denver would predict Debbie's diagnosis of cancer; and during the nineteen months that she battled cancer, Denver and Ron became closer than ever. Denver showed up on their doorstep every morning offering words of faith.

On the day Debbie died, Denver showed up on their doorstep and informed her that that was the day she would meet God. Denver shared with Ron that God said Debbie was holding on to make sure that the homeless would be taken care of in her absence. Throughout her sickness, Debbie would still go down to the homeless shelter and do makeovers for the women. She was committed to caring for the homeless, and Denver gave her the message to let her know it was okay to go. "I know you don't know who's gonna take care of them, the homeless. But God told me last night, he said, 'Denver, you tell Miss Debbie to lay down her torch and you pick it up for the rest of your life.'" After Debbie passed, Denver moved in with Ron, and the two of them lived together for the next eleven years, until Denver joined Debbie in heaven.

Ron says this story "was all based on an act of forgiveness that she showed me. It was the greatest gift she gave me. She never mentioned my affair again, until the very last day, when she died." Just a few days before Debbie passed away, she lay on her bed, with her kids and her husband by her side, and told them that she was releasing her husband to remarry and be with whomever he wanted after she was gone, and she asked her kids to honor that, too. Ron knows that his and his wife's love story could have ended in a very different way, "because we came to a point where we had to make a decision to love each other and stay with each other. Because of that forgiveness, we've now raised over a hundred million dollars for the homeless across America. It's a story grounded in that one act of forgiveness, because had she not given me or shown me that forgiveness, I would've run off with another woman and it would've been a very different story—one of the saddest stories ever told."

Ron still reflects on being given the gift of forgiveness with a sense of awe. He says that it took him about a year to really believe his wife had forgiven him, but he always felt her love and kindness throughout their journey together. Ron also reflects on the times he had to practice forgiveness in his friendship with Denver, when the older man would try to hit him or yell at him. All the work Debbie did with the homeless, and the work Ron continues to do, would not exist without forgiveness.

Ron sees Denver as a spiritual savant. When they first met, Ron knew Denver had not really connected with anyone in more than twenty-five years, except from a place of anger. He would then go on to become Ron's best friend. He knows that their friendship is all thanks to the Christlike forgiveness he received from Debbie. Her simple act of saying, "I will never bring this up again. You are forgiven," changed the course of Ron's life forever.

When Denver spoke at Debbie's funeral, he talked about the presence of Christ in her: "I was a bad man, a bad person. I didn't deserve love. But some very unlikely person came up and showed me love. I didn't wanna be friends with any white ladies, but she was so different. The longer I got to know her, I found out that everybody's different. The same kind of different as me. We just all regular folks walking down the road that God done put in front of us." Debbie and Ron's open embrace of Denver showed him how connected we all are, whatever our circumstances. As Denver said, "Whether we's rich or whether we's poor, or something in between, this earth ain't no final resting place. So in a way, we all are homeless, just working our way home."

I wanted to include Ron's experience not only because it's a remarkable story in itself, but because it is told by someone on the receiving end of forgiveness—someone who didn't necessarily feel that he deserved it. Many of us have been lucky enough to be at the receiving end of being forgiven for an act that we were sure we would be forever punished for. Hearing Ron's story made me reconsider how I think about receiving forgiveness, since the way that Debbie forgave Ron completely allowed him to alter the direction of his life. Going forward, when I am forgiven, I know that I'll think more deeply about how I might redirect my actions in the future for the better—to see it as an opportunity to embrace making a positive change for others around me.

Deborah Copaken

Confronting the Beast

"... Surely it is much more generous to forgive
and remember, than to forgive and forget."

—*Maria Edgeworth*

The night before Deborah Copaken graduated from college in 1988, she was out celebrating with friends. She accepted a ride home from one of the young men, not aware of how intoxicated he was. At approximately two a.m., the man raped her and passed out on her bed. Knowing she had a graduation ceremony to attend in a matter of hours, she sat on the floor, rocking herself at the foot of her bed, horrified at what had just happened. She showered, then waited for her rapist to wake up. When he finally awoke, he wrote his number down on a Post-it on her desk, told her he'd had a good time, and said she should give him a call sometime to see him again. Deb sat in utter shock and disbelief that her rapist could walk out of her room so casually, leaving his number like that for her to call. Traumatized, she grabbed her cap and gown and stumbled wearily out the door to her graduation ceremony.

It wasn't until thirty years later that Deb would revisit this incident and reach out to her rapist. The trigger was the September 2018 congressional hearing involving Dr. Christine Blasey Ford and Supreme Court nominee Brett Kavanaugh. Deb watched the proceedings as Ford documented her memories of sexual assault by Kavanaugh. When it was over, Deb sat down at her computer and began writing an email to the man who had assaulted her so many years ago. "I've been meaning to reach out to my rapist forever. I've been meaning to reach out to him for as long as I've been an adult, and it just seemed like the right time to do that. My thirtieth college reunion was coming up, and sometimes specific dates can seem like good benchmarks for fixing what's broken." Deb wrote to her rapist, describing the damage he had done, expecting nothing in return. Though she longed for an apology, she didn't think that it would come. Yet that was exactly what she received twenty minutes later. He called her on her cell phone—she'd given him her number in her email—and said that he had been so drunk he barely remembered the evening. He did remember thinking that the attraction had been mutual, but he now saw that what he did was terribly wrong. Most importantly, he said he was sorry. "The fact that he said such a hearty and contrite 'I'm sorry' was enormous," she explains. "It made me break down in tears immediately. I don't usually break down like that, but when he said, 'I'm sorry,' I immediately felt the sense of forgiveness." The weight of the rape that Deb had been carrying around for almost thirty years was suddenly lifting.

For Deb, the process of writing the email to her rapist "was 90 percent of the journey. The act of sitting down, writing this letter, and, my God, pressing send. That was the scariest moment—just hitting the send button." When her rapist called her phone minutes later, she was left speechless. "I'm still in shock at the grace of that act, and I still don't have words to describe how I felt. It's impossible, and I don't usually lack the words. I'm a writer. Words are my stock and trade. But I don't even have the proper words to express the sense of relief, because it's so much more than relief." Her feelings had been heard and addressed, all in a matter of minutes. Words like "validation," "relief," and "grace" came to mind, she said, "but those are all just words. It's like trying to describe love. 'Love' is a good word for love, but what else is love? It's hard to explain what love is, right?" Hearing her rapist apologize on the phone with genuine sincerity and contrition, Deb felt as if she had been taken back to her twenty-two-year-old self and cleansed of the pain of that haunting night. "When I wrote that letter, it was for me to forgive my twenty-two-year-old scared, wounded, traumatized self, who had dropped the ball and just moved on with her life because she didn't know how else to proceed. In many ways, the act of forgiveness was to myself." This is often the case when victims confront the task of forgiving—however difficult it may be to forgive their abuser, it may be even harder to forgive themselves for having hidden the pain and suffered silently for so long.

Another trigger that caused Deb to send this letter to her rapist was the time of year: it was on the eve of Yom Kippur, "the holiest of holy nights for Jews." On this holiday, "you forgive, and you both ask for forgiveness and forgive everyone else." This annual tradition of forgiveness is a beautiful gift that many give to themselves and to others, clearing their lives of the pain and resentment they may have been quietly carrying. For Deb, it meant saying, "The past is the past, and I want to move on. Sometimes, when we want to put the past to bed, we actually need to take stock of what's been done to us or what we've done to others." By forgiving, we move forward freely, unburdened by the past.

Deb credits her father with teaching her about forgiveness at a young age, leaving a lasting impression that has helped her get through some of life's most challenging times. Whenever she would talk to her father about an experience that was challenging for her, he would say, "You must forgive. You must allow them to say they're sorry, and even if they don't say they're sorry, you must show compassion to the bully. You must show compassion to this person who's hurting your feelings." Being able to forgive, regardless of the attitude of the person who has abused or wronged you, provides a path forward, free of the yoke of bitterness and resentment.

Deb openly shared her experience of confronting her rapist in an article for *The Atlantic*, and it had a larger ripple effect than she could have ever imagined. As her story spread, she received a flood of praise for having been so courageous and compassionate in reaching out to her rapist. She responded, saying, "No, I am preserving my sanity. For me, forgiving both him and this horrific incident was important for my own sense of well-being and my own emotional integrity."

Deb was surprised at the overwhelming reaction her story received. Her inbox was flooded with messages from both men and women telling her their stories and asking her for advice on how to move forward. She decided that she would publish the letter she wrote to her rapist on her website with the hopes that others would learn from her journey. She learned that "forgiveness between two people seems like a private act, like a very one-on-one exchange. But in fact, it becomes exponential, meaning other people start thinking about who they might need to apologize to or receive apologies from, and you set in motion this sort of ball of joy or forgiveness or whatever you want to call it that starts rolling down a hill." Seeing the chain reaction of people around her—some of whom she knew and some of whom she didn't—made the experience even more meaningful. The remarkable reaction to her act of forgiveness has strengthened her sense of optimism.

As Deb says, "So many things in this world don't work, but I can guarantee you: forgiveness does."

Reflecting on her journey, Deb believes that the timing was crucial. She looks back on the thirty years she carried the weight of her rape and feels that the letter she sent and the subsequent apology she was compassionately given arrived in her life at the time when she was able to receive and accept it. She realized, she says, that "your life is either about forgiveness or it's not. You're either a person who decides to accept others, warts and all, or you're a person who has difficulties maintaining friendships."

Forgiveness has allowed Deb to embrace a person who had haunted her for years. After she received his apology, she "was able to see him as a human again" instead of as a monster. This revelation has also changed the way she views others. She has learned to be more compassionate and more receptive to recognizing that we are all "human and flawed, and able to have relationships with these flawed humans" despite those flaws. When someone harms her, either intentionally or by accident, she has learned "that holding on to those feelings is only hurting yourself." When Deb sees others trapped in resentment, she asks them, "What are you afraid of if you forgive them? What would be the harm in forgiving?" And she tells them, from her own experience: "If you don't forgive someone, whoever it is who wronged you, that anger and that toxicity will poison you."

Deb's story brings hope to anyone wondering if they will ever get to a place of acceptance. We all need to go at our own pace, to have faith that one day we will have that same courage to sit down and write an email to someone who has wronged us, detailing those wrongs with the express purpose of giving them the chance to apologize and make it right. In return, both parties are then able to receive the gift of forgiveness.

Many people say that forgiveness came to them in an instant. Others say it took weeks, or months, even years. For Deb, it took thirty years. When she told me her story, I asked if she ever wished that she had forgiven her rapist sooner. She told me that it came at the perfect time for her.

Many of us feel a need to rush into forgiveness, to brush painful events quickly into the past. But forgiveness doesn't work unless you are ready to forgive. Deb's story teaches us that there is no time limit to forgiveness. It comes when you're ready, and it's never too late either to make amends or to ask for an apology. Hearing about her experience was a revelation to me, as it forced me to take inventory of my own grudges and take stock of situations in my past that I had been too raw or too afraid to confront when the feelings were still fresh. Stories like Deb's remind us that it's never too late to forgive.

Nadia Bolz-Weber

Pastor of Freedom

"Embrace the lessons when you finally learn
them, forgive yourself for what you did not know
earlier, and move forward in grace and peace and
self-compassion."

—*Elizabeth Gilbert*

At twenty-two years old, Nadia Bolz-Weber attended her first Alcoholics Anonymous meeting, resigned to the fact that she would be dead by thirty. When she joined AA, getting sober felt like "a rude interruption to my life." Yet she was able to get sober once she embraced the presence and power of God in her life. Nadia was led down a road of recovery by her Lutheran faith, a faith that taught her that we are all both sinner and saint.

In 2004, Nadia was asked to lead her friend's memorial service, as she was one of the only members of her circle with a religious affiliation. While conducting the service, she realized that so many of the people in the room—and in the world—would be judged as imperfect in most other religious places. These people needed a pastor to help guide them, and Nadia would be that pastor. In 2008, she was ordained by the Lutheran Church and founded the House for All Sinners and Saints, in Denver, Colorado.

Nadia's ministry is founded on her own journey through addiction and recovery, self-abuse and self-forgiveness. Although she modestly refers to herself as the "I-suck-at-forgiveness-and-I'm-desperate pastor," her past weaknesses make her all the more compassionate to the needs of her congregation. She is familiar with the struggle to forgive, and she remembers a time when she, too, felt imprisoned by resentment.

Nadia's path to forgiveness was shaped by her experiences in the twelve-step program. In the AA community, she learned about the dangers of holding on to resentment, the "dubious luxury of ordinary men." To help lead recovering alcoholics away from resentment and toward forgiveness, she addresses the part of the AA program that encourages people to identify and accept their own role in whatever hurt they have experienced. As she points out, many of us feel that acknowledging the way we have participated in the hurt feels "like a betrayal of the hurt." But looking critically at our role in it is a key step to forgiving and living a life free of the burden of resentment.

The "Big Book" of Alcoholics Anonymous, AA's primary text on recovery from substance abuse, also talks about reflecting on our life events to pinpoint when it was that we "made a decision based on self that put us in a position to be harmed." To illustrate this principle, Nadia uses the example of being able to reunite with her ex-boyfriend. When her boyfriend broke up with her, she felt destroyed. Twenty-two years later, they rekindled their relationship. Now they have been back together for more than two years. One day recently, while they were on a plane together, her boyfriend asked her how she had been able to forgive him for leaving her. She told him she had finally reached a place where "I was able to be honest about how much of my own suffering in that situation was of my own making."

When you are able to take responsibility for your own role in a painful situation—even if it's just a small portion of the responsibility—it allows you to "detach the person." For most of us, looking at our own role in a painful situation can feel strange and unnatural. As Nadia says, "I know why it's hard for us—because it feels like we're betraying our hurt self. Like it's an act of treason against my injured self for me to cut that chain of resentment toward the person who was involved. But it's not. It's actually honoring my whole self enough to say, 'We're gonna move on now. We're not gonna be attached to you anymore. We're gonna move on.'"

Recasting your story is one of the keys of breaking free from the past. We must abandon the victim narrative and become our own protagonist. As Nadia says, "We get so attached to the story we're telling that we just think, 'It's true, and it's the only one that can be true.' But, oh my gosh, no; you can actually tell the story in different ways—ways that are still true and that still honor who you are and your hurt, but that don't keep you in that place." The real courage comes when you make the decision to really separate yourself from the incident. "If we have this story we're telling about our own victimhood, what's the payoff to that? To really move on requires so much bravery and so much truth-telling and so much letting go. It can be a lot easier to just stay in that shitty place and continue to feel bad for ourselves. But that's not freedom."

Nadia stresses the importance of separating your feelings toward someone who has harmed you and the pain you've experienced as a result. She explains, "I think the key is to understand the difference between the person and the hurt we're experiencing. What we do is, we feel pain, we feel hurt, we feel injury, we feel resentment, we feel anger, we have all those feelings of betrayal and whatnot—and then we stitch those together with the person. And so many times, the feelings are of a larger size than can be attributed directly just to the action of a person." Although your feelings of pain and injury may be valid, if you allow yourself to stay in that pattern of suffering, it becomes a vicious cycle. Nadia states, "It's important to honor the hurt, the injury, the pain. I'm not saying dismiss it. I'm just saying detach it from the human as much as you can. Because as long as the feeling of hurt and pain is attached to another person, it's going to be so much more difficult to heal from the harm." Once we take responsibility for our anguish, we become responsible for the healing. While others may have participated in the hurt, we must take ownership of the healing of that pain in order to move forward.

The ability to live a truly free life requires "breaking that chain that is binding us to that person." Nadia likens this process to using bolt cutters to break free of the people who are forcing you to carry around anger and hate. And those bolt cutters are forgiveness—forgiveness that severs the ties from that person and that pain. You don't have to ever trust them again, but you can free yourself from carrying around the baggage of anger toward them. Releasing that anger can feel like a sacrifice. It may be tempting to cling to an old wound and judge our enemy. But when we focus on the wrong that has been done to us, it only provides us with momentary satisfaction. "I gain nothing," Nadia explains. "It feels good, but it's a sugar high, it's self-righteousness. It feels good for a moment."

Having past experiences reemerge and upset you doesn't mean that you haven't forgiven. What has helped Nadia when such feelings arise is trying to see the situation from the perspective of the person who harmed her. Allowing yourself to express compassion for the other person can change your feelings of judgment, not only for the person but also for yourself. She says that while "we can hold people accountable for the harm that their actions cause, we can also have compassion for how they ended up in the position to choose that." We all have reasons why we behave in certain ways. This doesn't excuse our behavior, but it explains it, and these explanations can guide the person who needs to forgive. Ultimately, forgiveness is a gift that you give yourself; it has little to do with the worthiness or well-being of the other person. As Nadia reminds us, "It's entirely to do with your own heart and your own being and your own blood pressure."

Forgiveness can be a long process. Nadia encourages us to be patient: "Sometimes it's not this once-and-done thing. Sometimes I have to go through the process again, even after I've reached a point of freedom from the resentment. It'll creep back in." When the resentment or anger does reemerge, it may be helpful to turn to a higher power. Nadia finds solace through prayer. She believes in "trying to connect to God. Because I just know I'm not enough."

Nadia also knows the power of receiving forgiveness. Throughout her life she has been forgiven by others—often when she did not feel worthy of forgiveness—and she has learned that it can bring about a "transformation of the human heart." She says, "It shifted something in me that nothing else could." She wants to be able to effect that kind of transformation in others because it's a "beautiful gift," one that is rare to give and rare to receive. It's one of the rare *healthy* addictions, and it has left her "desperate for freedom, desperate to share this life-transforming gift with others." Being a "desperate human" allowed her to dig deep and explore and gain a better understanding of forgiveness and how it plays out in her life. Nadia thinks that forgiveness is something we practice throughout our entire lives; it never has an ending point. And it has become her lifelong mission. Once we discover the power of forgiveness, the only time we will stop forgiving is with "our final breath."

Nadia has been on both sides of forgiveness; she's given it and received it, and she knows how powerful it can be. She talks about forgiveness not as a sign of weakness, but as a declaration that, no matter how wrong something was that happened to you, you can choose to cut ties with it. Nadia calls those who forgive "freedom fighters." Her perspective gives power to the forgiver, and it allowed me to look at my own experiences with forgiveness in a different way. For so long, I had seen forgiveness as a form of surrender—a way to move beyond a painful incident while avoiding conflict. If a friend hurt me, I would say, "I forgive you," and hope that that would magically make everything okay between us. Now, visualizing forgiveness as a form of strength instead has changed my view completely. It is not an invitation for others to harm you; it's the act of taking back your power and freeing yourself from your past.

Lewis Howes

Mindful Masculinity

> "And it is only when we grant ourselves mercy
> that we can extend this mercy to others."
>
> —*Mary Pipher*

Lewis Howes is a former professional football player, internationally acclaimed *New York Times* bestselling author, entrepreneur, and social media expert. As the host of the podcast *The School of Greatness*, he delivers messages of hope and inspiration to audiences across the nation. So few would have guessed that he was haunted by dark events in his past—events that would overshadow his success and leave him trapped in a cage of anger and resentment. Only once he was able to reveal the abuse he had suffered and forgive his abuser was Lewis finally able to discover the inner peace that he had long been craving.

But the path toward that peace was not easy, especially when it came to forgiving himself. As Lewis says, "I used to beat myself up for everything. For feeling insignificant, for feeling stupid, for feeling like I'd messed things up with my parents, for them getting divorced, for my siblings having struggles." When he finally learned to forgive himself, he discovered that it was "one of the most powerful things." This realization came after a series of personal hardships forced him to confront his lingering past.

At the age of thirty, Lewis "went through a lot of different transitions in my life." He was experiencing the end of an intimate relationship and the dissolving of a business partnership, he was involved in a brutal physical fight during a basketball game, and he broke ties with several close friends. As he considered these setbacks, he recognized that the one thing they all had in common was him: "I was at the baseline of every one of these relationships." Finally, when his best friend from college told him that he didn't want to hang out with him anymore, Lewis finally had to confront his inner demons. "On the outside it looked like I had it all. I was making millions of dollars. But on the inside, I was suffering. I had zero inner peace. I didn't know how to get it. I didn't know how to find peace inside." Lewis eventually discovered that practicing forgiveness was the essential element that he needed in order to achieve that inner peace. As he says, "If you're resenting someone, or resenting yourself, you're gonna be living with this sense of suffering—a lack of inner peace—and always fighting it." Lewis wanted to make a change, but first he had to figure out where all the turmoil in his life was coming from. So he started a course of therapy and attended various workshops.

It wasn't until Lewis decided to open up about the sexual abuse he had experienced as a child that things really began to shift. It was a secret that he had hidden for decades. Finally, twenty-five years later, he was able to tell the full story, from start to finish, in front of his men's group. "I wasn't really sure what would happen when I opened up about it, but I was terrified that if anyone knew this about me, then no one would love me anymore."

Growing up in the Midwest, Lewis felt that "it was unacceptable to be abused, or to look weak, or to be taken advantage of. It was always a defense mechanism, to be more aggressive." But the work he had done in therapy and workshops gave him the confidence he needed to be honest about his past. When he finished telling the story, he started sobbing. He became so emotional that he excused himself from the group to breathe. While he was sitting outside, recovering from reliving the trauma of his childhood, the men from his group came outside, one by one, to comfort him. "They kept saying, 'You're my hero.'" Several men told him that they, too, had experienced similar abuse, and Lewis's ability to be open about his past helped them heal. "That changed everything for me, the reactions of the men in the room. They trusted me more, they loved me more, they respected me more. I thought it would be the complete opposite." Sharing the story of his abuse in front of the members of his men's group—most of whom he didn't know all that well—allowed Lewis to be open about his abuse for the first time with his close friends and family. He could finally say, "I forgive this person who did this to me, and I forgive myself for beating myself up for all these years." He was able to let go of the shame and bitterness he'd been harboring throughout his life. He realized that forgiveness is about being vulnerable and being true to who you are. It's about allowing your mask of masculinity to come off and letting your true self heal.

As Lewis began his journey of forgiveness, he noticed immediate improvements in his life. He no longer experienced the "anxiety or the stress, the worry that I had always slept with. I was able to have peace." The rejuvenation that Lewis experienced was not only emotional, but also physical: "My health has transformed in the last five years through the act of forgiveness, because with forgiveness comes freedom."

Forgiveness also transformed Lewis's relationships with others. As he told me, "If I'm holding a grudge, then I'm not only hurting myself; I'm hurting everyone else around me by expressing negativity as opposed to being positive and being of help to people. I think it's our mission to be of service at the highest level." Lewis says that doing the work to arrive at a place of forgiveness can be uncomfortable, but it's the key to breaking free. The hardest part for him was confronting the abuse that had triggered his resentment. After that, he found forgiving others to be relatively easy. As he says, "In the work, I had a willingness. I forgave everyone else."

Lewis has forgiven his abuser and has moved on with his life, but he still views the act of forgiveness as an ongoing process that he continues to work on. When he experiences a "trigger" moment—such as hearing an account of abuse—he uses it as "a reminder to follow through on the practices that I have: meditation, mindfulness, breathing, working out, all these things. And awareness—it's going through it again and taking a moment, then going back to normal life, as opposed to holding on to resentment and anger. Because I've lived that for a long time, and it just doesn't work for me anymore."

Learning how to forgive came with time and experience for Lewis. But once he embraced the practice, he found that it entered every part of his life, even allowing him to reconcile with his estranged brother. When Lewis was eight years old, his brother went to jail for selling drugs to an undercover cop. During that time, Lewis became alienated from his friends, because the neighborhood parents thought he might be criminally inclined like his brother. He remembers feeling deeply upset toward his brother—as if his brother had robbed him of his childhood. Since then, Lewis has forgiven his brother and no longer carries that resentment.

Lewis has found that fully embracing forgiveness in every facet of his life is the only way to live free of resentment. As he says, "I feel like you don't understand forgiveness unless you can forgive everything that's happened. If you hold on to a grudge for one person or one incident in your life, but you forgive other things, I don't think you've truly forgiven. You're either all in on forgiveness or you're holding on to a grudge." By holding on to negative energy for one person or one situation, "there's going to be this toxic poison in your body and your heart for that one person, every single moment of the day, because you're holding on to that. You haven't truly forgiven unless you can forgive everything. It's a daily practice. We can hold a grudge all the time, or we can choose to constantly live in forgiveness and be at peace."

In order to fully embrace this wisdom, Lewis starts every day in meditation, preparing himself for anything that might upset him. In this way, he shields himself from the inevitable insults and accidents that could otherwise ruin his day. While it is important to feel all the emotions you are going through, it is equally important to eventually release them and not allow them to lock you in a state of negativity. "When you hold on to that grudge, you're essentially saying that that person has power over you. You're giving them your power. When you forgive that person, you take your power back. You say, 'This person no longer has power over me. I'm not going to give them my energy. I'm not going to give them all my time, my thoughts, my feelings. I'm going to take my power back by forgiving them. Not for them, but for me.'"

Even though holding on to a grudge might seem easier at

times, forgiving is the only way to take your power back and be set free. "The more you hold on to a grudge, the more you're just hurting yourself and your dreams. You're hurting the people around you even more. That person who you aren't forgiving now affects you, your family, your friends, your coworkers, and everyone else around you. They have power and control over everyone else, too, because you're allowing them to have control over you." As Lewis points out, forgiving someone does not mean that you condone the person's actions or allow them back into your life. Forgiving is a way to release your pain and bitterness and move forward with a mind uncluttered by rage and resentment. "It's holding them accountable still, but allowing yourself off the hook of feeling anger, rage, and pain."

Talking to Lewis also reminded me that, too often, we make the mistake of comparing ourselves to others. We wonder why we don't look as happy as others do or why we aren't as successful, etc. Hearing Lewis's story is a great reminder that what you see on the outside does not always reflect what's happening on the inside. Sometimes, people who chase after perfection are running from demons that we know nothing about. Lewis was able to free himself through a process of forgiveness, and that process has become a daily practice. His story reminded me of the importance of withholding judgment; we're all humans, all flawed, all struggling, all doing our best. Life is hard enough without the burden of guilt and judgment; we should remind ourselves from time to time to be a little more compassionate—with others and with ourselves.

Scarlett Lewis

Healing Love

> "Never does the human soul appear so strong as
> when it foregoes revenge, and dares to forgive an
> injury."
>
> —*Edwin Hubbell Chapin*

Scarlett Lewis vividly remembers seeing her son Jesse for the last time. Long before losing her son, she had made a decision to be a present parent. As a single mom to two boys, Scarlett knew the immense value of being actively involved in her sons' lives. With their time together hemmed in by early mornings at school and evening drop-offs at soccer practice, she wanted their time at home to be free of distraction from television or video games. On the morning of December 14, 2012, Scarlett remembers walking Jesse to the curb where his father, Neil, was picking him up. Scarlett was talking to her son's father, caught up in the hectic morning rush. When she turned around to give her son a hug good-bye, she saw that he had written "I love you" in the frost of her car with his finger. Knowing that this was a moment to remember, Scarlett ran inside to get her camera and took a picture of Jesse standing by the car. Little did Scarlett know that that would be the last picture ever taken of her son.

Jesse attended Sandy Hook Elementary School. When Scarlett was notified of the shooting, she waited at the firehouse with her mother and her other son, J.T., desperate for information. Jesse was not among the kids who'd come walking out of the school, one by one, escorted by police. Scarlett spoke to the officers, who asked her if she had any recent pictures of Jesse and if he had an identifying marks. As she waited in the cold evening air, she felt J.T.'s eyes on her, watching every move she made, listening to every word that came from her mouth. "I knew that, in that moment, the way I handled this, regardless of the outcome, was going to shape the way that J.T. handled trauma, tragedy, difficulty, challenges, and roadblocks for the rest of his life." Knowing this helped Scarlett stay strong, and ultimately helped her to forgive. Scarlett wanted the same for J.T. "I wanted him to have a forgiving heart, because what I've grown to learn is that, in some cases, that is the only way to take back your power."

When Scarlett was told that Jesse had been killed, her world imploded. She went to her mother's house, because the idea of returning to her home—the last place she'd seen her son alive—was too gut-wrenching. Reeling in grief, she tried to grasp how something so cruel and senseless could have happened. "I remember right off the bat thinking that whoever could do something so horrendous must have been in a tremendous amount of pain. And that turned out to be true."

Scarlett recalled going back to her house for the first time to get clothes for her son to be buried in. She gathered items from his dresser drawer, and as she was passing through the kitchen, she noticed a message he had left on their kitchen chalkboard. "Jesse, shortly before he died—no one saw him do this—wrote three words: 'nurturing, healing, love.' I stopped when I saw that, and I knew instantly that if Adam Lanza, the shooter, had been able to give and receive nurturing, healing, and love, the tragedy would never have happened. It's pretty simple. And it was in that way that I started to feel compassion for him. If you're connected to other people, you don't want to harm them." Sensing that her son might have had a premonition, Scarlett wanted to find the deeper meaning in her son's message and help spread it.

Scarlett reached out to Dr. Chris Kukk, a professor at Western Connecticut State University who has done extensive research into compassion. She showed Dr. Kukk Jesse's message and explained her vision to spread it. Dr. Kukk later told her that those three words—nurturing, healing, love—"are in the definition of compassion across all cultures. Nurturing means loving kindness, healing means forgiveness, and love is compassion in action—so it's the identification of the need or suffering in another and the acting to do something to help ease that pain." Just a few days after the shooting, Scarlett discovered that her son had actually saved the lives of nine of his classmates before losing his own. Learning of the courage that he displayed has given her the strength to forgive.

Forgiving Adam Lanza was a vital step in Scarlett's healing process. She had compassion for him from the start, after sensing that his actions had been motivated by deep turmoil. While she allowed herself time to process the death of her son, she knew the way to forgiveness would be to humanize Lanza.

In March 2013, a few months after her son's death, Scarlett founded the Jesse Lewis Choose Love Movement, with the mission to help spread the message of forgiveness among people suffering from loss. While doing this work, Scarlett has met people who knew Adam who said that he had experienced severe bullying. The more Scarlett learned about Adam, the more she came to appreciate that he was a child whose needs simply hadn't been met. "Adam literally did everything he was supposed to do as a little boy"—but the time, attention, and resources he needed were not provided to him. She learned that when Adam was in first grade, he handed out birthday invitations at school, but no one showed up to his party. When he was in fifth grade, he wrote an essay titled "The Book of Granny," illustrating a witch coming to school with a broomstick that turned into a semiautomatic weapon to murder the students. "That is a young person crying out for help, not knowing any other way to do it." Scarlett chooses to view Adam's mounting rage from a compassionate perspective—as a child isolated from his peers, veering toward violence because of the pain he suffered. Feeling empathy for Adam has allowed her to release the anger she felt toward him and redirect that anger *for* him. "Reading some reports that he had needs that were not met, that he was neglected—and neglect, in my mind, is the worst form of bullying—I can honestly say, it's easier for me to be angry for him than to be angry at him."

The loss of her son has given Scarlett a much deeper appreciation for the process of forgiving. "I did start out feeling compassion for him. I didn't know anything about forgiveness, by the way. I was raised Christian; we talked about the need to forgive. But we're not told what that means for the forgiver, the benefits to the forgiver, how to do it. And so it did start with a feeling of compassion for the shooter. However, you look at your son's dead body in the casket for the first time—his tiny light casket, and your six-year-old son lying in it, with a bullet hole through his forehead—and you feel a tremendous amount of anger."

Scarlett recalls Jesse's seventh birthday, six months after his death. She planned a big celebration, with the blow-up slide that he had begged her for when he was still alive. She wanted to celebrate his life. On the morning of the party, she woke up distraught, paralyzed by the thought of celebrating her son's birthday without him. The anger welled up inside her again—anger for the shooter who took her son from her. "I think we love to blame when something happens to us. The first thing we say normally is, 'Oh, whose fault is this? Who can I blame?' And of course Adam Lanza and his mom were the natural targets, because, well, Adam was the perpetrator and his mom gave him the gun. Yes, he's responsible for the tragedy; however, is it really all his fault?" Scarlett realized that it would be easy for her to stay angry at Adam and his mother, but they weren't wholly to blame.

Scarlett learned that Adam's mother had taken him to Sandy Hook Elementary as a kindergartner. He was tested, and it was determined that he needed special services, which he was then denied. Scarlett had many striking similarities with Lanza's mother. Scarlett, too, had taken J.T. for testing at Sandy Hook, and he, too, was denied special services. Both Scarlett and Adam's mother were single moms, and Scarlett knew the struggle to connect with a teenage son. The mistake Adam's mother made was connecting with him over a gun.

Rather than shifting all the blame onto the Lanzas, Scarlett chose to look at the incident more broadly and examine her own role in a society that allowed this incident to occur. "I take my part of the responsibility for what's happening in our schools and in our society. I lived in the town that cultivated Adam Lanza; he had a lifetime of pain. Did I ever cross his path? I don't think so. But I know we're all incredibly powerful. How we treat each other manifests in so many different ways. And there's a ripple effect—there truly is. And if we don't all start taking responsibility for what's going on, we're never going to fix it."

The only way Scarlett could attend her son's birthday party was to take a deep breath and forgive again. "Forgiveness starts with a choice, and then it becomes a process. It's taking your personal power back. That's my new and improved definition." She realized she could get through this ordeal by taking her personal power back and choosing not to allow herself to be the victim. "If I did not forgive Adam, it would give him power over my thoughts, which affect my feelings, which then affect my behavior. It's called the cognitive triangle in the mental health field. I would literally be giving him control over me, and I would become another victim of the Sandy Hook shooting. And probably that would have induced J.T. to become another victim as well. Instead, I chose to forgive."

Having empathy for Adam allowed Scarlett to become part of the solution. In her journey, she learned that there are two kinds of people in this world: "There are good people who want to be part of the solution, who are trying to implement social and emotional learning, and then there are good people in pain. And that's what I see Adam Lanza as. Did he want to grow up to be a mass murderer? No way. That was the result of neglect and pain and disconnection. If we had given him the skills and the tools to be able to choose a better, happier path, doesn't it make sense he would have chosen that?"

Scarlett was first able to put her journey of forgiveness into words after a profoundly moving experience with her son J.T. In the wake of the shooting, J.T. was reluctant to go back to school. Each day, Scarlett would ask him if he was ready, and he would say no, choosing to stay home another day. On the one hand, she was relieved that her son was at home, where he would be safe; on the other hand, she knew that he needed to go back to school and finish seventh grade. His counselors suggested he repeat the grade, but she didn't want him to feel punished for taking time to grieve. It wasn't until a group of orphaned genocide survivors from Rwanda reached out to J.T. on Skype that there was a shift for both Scarlett and her son. Put in touch through a family connection, these survivors told J.T. on-screen: "We heard about what happened to your little brother all the way over here in Rwanda, and we're so terribly sorry. We want you to know that you're going to be okay, and you will feel joy again." Then the orphans shared their stories from the genocide: some had lost families, some had been attacked, some had nearly starved to death. A girl named Chantelle had been just eight years old when her neighbors murdered her family and slit her throat. They buried her in a shallow grave where she lay for days, hiding until she finally dug herself out and made her way to an orphanage. The survivors told J.T. that they'd realized "they had to forgive, and if they didn't forgive, they'd go down the same path as the killers." They also told him that they have been able to find meaning in their suffering by being able to reach out to people, like J.T., who have experienced loss, and help them on their journey.

It was after that call that J.T. decided he would go back to school. Scarlett and her son sat and talked about the impact of that Skype call. They made a gratitude list. "We had a lot to be grateful for. And then we both made the commitment to forgive. We voiced it to each other." J.T. went back to school the next day and started an organization to raise money to help Rwandan genocide survivors attend university. "The takeaway from that story is that when we made the commitment to forgive, J.T. turned around and wanted to send out the love that those kids had given to him. I feel like that strengthened him to do that. And he's still doing it. The nurturing, healing, love that you give out, you get back."

Scarlett explained to me that part of the Jesse Lewis Choose Love Movement is to offer a "no-cost comprehensive social and emotional learning program, pre-K through twelfth grade. Teaching kids forgiveness is a big part of the program, because forgiveness was the most important part of my journey of healing. And it's the only reason that I am able to travel around and do what I do in the Choose Love Movement." Scarlett says it's important to teach our children about forgiveness at a young age. Throughout her journey, traveling around and growing the program, she has learned that kids are surprisingly well versed in forgiveness. "Forgiveness is something that kids use a lot. It's the adults who don't understand it. Forgiveness is so vitally important for our society to continue." She noted that forgiveness often happens to be the students' favorite character value, and when asked why, they respond, "Because it feels so good to let go. It's like a superpower!" Convinced that the world would be a different place had forgiveness been taught in schools earlier, Scarlett works hard to spread the message in schools today. Helping children learn about social emotional learning is an important way to prevent kids from hurting one another. "Teaching kids how to get along, how to be resilient, how to manage their emotions—that's cultivating safety from the inside out." In 2018, Scarlett helped New Hampshire governor Chris Sununu and his director of homeland security, Perry Plummer, pass a statewide school initiative focusing on social and emotional learning as part of school safety.

Being able to understand the roots of Adam Lanza's need to lash out against others allowed Scarlett to take her power back and move forward. Forgiveness has given Scarlett the ability to find meaning in her loss and transform her grief into action that has helped the lives of many others.

Scarlett's story shows us the power of forgiveness to transform tragedy into positive change. There was nothing obvious about Scarlett's choice to forgive, and yet she knew immediately that it was her only path forward. Clinging to grief and blame would have trapped her forever in her darkest moment. Many people I know have used anger as a way to cope with trauma because the idea of letting it go is too painful for them to face. I've been there, too. After hearing Scarlett's story, though, I'm inspired to find a way to recalibrate in those moments of anger—to release negative emotions in favor of positive action. I have found that it's helpful to remember that even if you don't feel ready to release anger toward someone, just taking that first small positive step can actually jolt you into the right frame of mind to get you on track to a lasting pathway to forgiveness.

In 2019, Scarlett's son J.T. announced he is running for the Connecticut State Senate to honor his little brother, Jesse, and focus on school safety policies.

DeVon Franklin

Releasing the Burden

"We must develop and maintain the capacity to forgive. He who is devoid of the power to forgive is devoid of the power to love."

—*Martin Luther King Jr.*

While DeVon Franklin has become a hugely successful producer, preacher, bestselling author, and motivational speaker, he, too, has struggled with learning and understanding the process of forgiveness. He has had to forgive family and friends along the way. Above all, changing his perspective on his troubled relationship with his father has helped him come out the other side stronger than ever before.

His journey with forgiveness began when his father, who struggled with alcoholism, passed away when DeVon was just nine years old. He grew up with a lot of anger toward his father for a variety of reasons, but primarily because, in most memories he has of his father, he was intoxicated. While his father was never physically abusive toward him, DeVon recalls him being an aggressive drunk. His heavy drinking and unhealthy lifestyle contributed to his sudden heart attack at thirty-six years old, and his absence left DeVon with a deep sense of emptiness. He felt as though his dad didn't "prepare him for life," which filled him with anger.

Unable to process this rage, DeVon channeled it toward the remaining authority figure in his life: his mother. When she wouldn't attend basketball games or school events, he would become even angrier. It was only later that he came to understand that his mother was missing those events because she was working to provide for her family as a single mother. "I used to really have a lot of resentment about that, and it wasn't until college when I began to realize that she did the best she could—and even my father did the best he could. Sometimes forgiveness can work that way, where you're holding a grudge against somebody and they may not even know what they did. And so, with my mother, she never did anything wrong, but in my adolescence I never understood the sacrifice of what she was doing." It was only later, when he realized why his mother had been absent, that he was able to forgive her and release the resentment he'd felt toward her. He was also able to let go of the anger he'd felt toward his father—an anger that he recognized was not serving him. As DeVon told me, "No matter how angry I may be, no matter how upset, reality is, he's gone. I'm still here."

The awareness that he needed to release his anger toward both his mother and father allowed DeVon to begin to heal. He didn't want the bitterness he felt toward his father to fill him with hate or push him toward becoming an alcoholic himself. "That really required me to offer forgiveness and say, 'I just got to let it go. Let me find something I can be grateful for.' I am grateful for him giving me life. I'm grateful that I at least have some memories of him." It was shifting his perspective and realizing what he was grateful for that allowed him to release the anger he'd been holding toward his father. Recognizing all the sacrifices his mother had made for him enabled DeVon to release that resentment as well, and has allowed them to have a close relationship today. "Today we have an incredible relationship, yet that all came because I had to alleviate the burden that I was carrying. And it wasn't easy, because sometimes we can find comfort in our anger, our frustration, our bitterness that comes from unforgiveness. Being able to process that and forgive and say, 'It's okay, it's okay.' She did the best she could and, as a matter of fact, he did the best he could. That revelation for me was very cathartic—it was very powerful and it was very liberating."

DeVon's healing process began when he realized that he was maintaining a distance that was preventing him from getting everything he wanted out of his relationships because he feared vulnerability. He would allow himself to get close to someone, but only to a certain degree. Losing his father at a young age had taught him the survival tactic of cutting off his emotions and his ability to feel vulnerable. The sadness he felt when he lost his father was something he never wanted to feel again, so he closed himself off from true intimacy. It wasn't until he met his future wife that he would allow himself to release his anger and become vulnerable in order to make the relationship work. "I think sometimes there's this misunderstanding of forgiveness. Sometimes people think, 'Oh, okay. You know what? I forgive—and all of a sudden that wound is magically healed.' Well, it's not. So I forgave my father, but that didn't mean I wasn't closed off. That didn't mean I wasn't afraid to be vulnerable. There was still a residual impact of that forgiveness that I still had to process and work through."

Being able to humanize his father during his healing process also helped DeVon ensure that he wouldn't continue to carry his anger forward. Discovering that his father's alcoholism may have stemmed from the fact that his father's father, mother, and siblings all struggled with alcoholism, too, allowed DeVon to put things into perspective and have empathy for his father's addiction.

While DeVon has forgiven his father for his weaknesses, he will never forget. "When something traumatic has happened to us, we may be able to forgive the person or the circumstance, but we never forget it. We never forget it. Why? Because it always stays with us." Being able to acknowledge the hurt is the first and most important step, but not forgetting is just as important. "I think the power of forgiveness can be found in not forgetting what has happened, but not allowing it to have a negative, long-term impact in our life, as much as we can control that." While some injuries might resonate more than others, the challenge is to make sure you carry a positive message moving forward.

Allowing ourselves the time we need to process the hurt is also critical; we need to be gentle on ourselves. DeVon explains, "No one should feel pressured to forgive prior to being ready to do so." He notes that, in certain communities, there is an expectation that after an incident occurs you should quickly move toward the forgiveness process. That may be unhealthy when you are still deeply feeling the hurt that you just experienced. He uses the analogy of getting hit by a car and someone telling you to stand up and walk already—but you can't do what you aren't ready to do. Taking the time you need to get to that process is vital. "It doesn't mean it should linger, however; too often I feel like we are not sympathetic enough to the person who needs to forgive. If I've been offended, it's for me to give the forgiveness; it's for me to feel ready to forgive. And it's okay sometimes to not be ready. It's okay to say, 'You know what? I'm still resentful. I'm still a little upset. And I know I gotta work through it, but for the moment I'm just gonna own how I feel.' Everyone has to feel ready in their spirit when they're ready to offer forgiveness." We often forget about the importance of being kind to ourselves—and others—during the healing process. The goal is to achieve forgiveness, but "it's important to not put a time constraint or to put pressure on someone if they just aren't there yet."

Whether we like it or not, it is often the fact that the person who has hurt us has moved on with their life that causes us to realize that we have not. "The challenge about not offering forgiveness," DeVon says, "is that many times the person who has offended has moved on with their life, for better or worse. But the one who is offended holds on to the pain in ways that can be severely detrimental to the entire course of their life." One of the most harmful consequences of holding on to pain is that we now carry the responsibility and burden with us, until we get to a place where we can alleviate it. "One of the challenges of forgiveness is that when I hold on to resentment, I am the one who bears the weight of it. So, while no one should be rushed to forgive, it's highly important to forgive as soon as you possibly can."

Time and experience have given DeVon a greater understanding of forgiveness. "If I forgive, that means that I have to be vulnerable, because I have to admit that something offended me. Everyone has a process. Forgiveness is complicated. It takes time. However, it doesn't stop me from encouraging people to do it—but it does stop me from judging if they don't."

Forgiveness is a process that can't be rushed. There have been times in my own life when I've forgiven too quickly, trying to sweep a painful incident under the rug. These incidents always left a bitter taste in my mouth, showing me that I wasn't yet ready to forgive. The concept of forgiving and not forgetting might sound negative—as if you haven't really moved on. But keeping a memory of whatever you granted forgiveness for is actually a great way to learn from your past, with the hope that you can then prevent whatever happened from repeating in your future.

By being patient with himself and forgiving his father fully, DeVon was able to break a generations-old cycle of addiction and neglect. As he so beautifully articulated, getting to a place of forgiveness takes work—often painful work, work we wish we could avoid. But if we don't take the time to confront our pain, we'll never be free of it.

Mark Rozzi

Faith Betrayed

"Forgiveness is giving up the hope that the past
could be any different. It's accepting the past for
what it was and using this moment and this time
to help yourself move forward."

—*Oprah Winfrey*

Mark Rozzi grew up in a small town in Pennsylvania. He
went to a private Catholic school attended mostly by
children from his Italian-American neighborhood. When he
was in seventh grade, he remembers hearing that his school
would be welcoming a charismatic new priest, Father Graff.
Mark knew that once he entered eighth grade, he would serve
under Father Graff at the church. He vividly remembers the
first interaction he had with the priest. He was sitting in the
church with his classmates one Friday morning as Father Graff
said mass. In the middle of the service, Mark remembers the
priest walking down the aisle and suddenly screaming at some-

one. He sat in shock, thinking that whoever the priest was yelling at must have done something terribly wrong. Then Father Graff turned, walked over to Mark's row, and began yelling at him. He felt humiliated and dumbfounded as to what he could have possibly done to deserve that kind of treatment. He had been sitting quietly throughout the church service.

After the service ended, Mark remembers his teacher telling him that he should stay to talk to Father Graff about what he had done. "I can remember going up. He put his arm around me and said that everything was going to be all right. It was like Dr. Jekyll and Mr. Hyde." Father Graff told Mark that he would help him get on the right path—he only had to listen to what the priest told him to do and everything would be okay. "I didn't want to disappoint him. I wanted to make sure that I showed him that I was this good kid. But I tell everybody— that's the day he had me. That's the day my grooming started." Mark soon began serving under Father Graff. He recalls being taken to various places with him. Since Graff was a big horse gambler, sometimes he would take Mark to buy horse racing magazines, other times to Penn National racetrack, where the priest "would take his collar out and turn into Uncle Eddie."

He remembers the first time the priest turned from church elder into full-blown predator. Father Graff was driving Mark back after one of their outings, and he invited him up to his residence, located on the second floor of the rectory. Father Graff sat Mark down on a couch and asked him if he wanted a beer, promising not to say a word. The beer led to videos containing pornography, which eventually led the priest to take Mark into a back room where he showed him more pornography. Then he removed Mark's pants, measured his penis, and took naked photographs of him. "He was keeping statistics so he could chart my growth. Of course, he would start to fondle me and play with me. And that happened a couple of times, under the guise of 'education.'" Shortly after, Mark discovered a dresser drawer in Graff's room filled with "Polaroids of a lot of my friends—tons of pictures of naked boys."

Mark vividly remembers his final episode with Father Graff. One Saturday, he and his friend Tom were serving mass. Afterward, Graff told the two boys to go back to his private room. They did as they were told. Father Graff handed them both beers, played pornographic movies, and then took each of them to the adjoining bedroom—first one at a time, and then together—to photograph them nude. Then Graff kept Mark in the bedroom and sent Tom back to the front room. Mark recalls, "I can remember him asking me what I knew about sex positions. He started putting me in these different sexual positions, and he ended by putting me in the sixty-nine position. Then he started performing oral sex on me and wanted me to reciprocate." When Mark declined, the priest became aggressive. He grabbed him and put him in the shower. He began touching Mark, then raping him. "I can remember focusing on a little tile on the wall, and I was just staring at this tile, and I just knew that I had one of two choices: I can either stand here and take this, or I'm going to run right now. And within that split second, I was like, I'm out of here." Mark and Tom ran out of the room, sprinting for their lives. As they fled, Father Graff yelled after them, warning them to keep their mouths shut.

Mark arrived home, breathless and terrified. His mother questioned him, but he refused to say anything. His mother took him to the principal's office the following Monday, trying to discover what was troubling her son from the Saturday mass. Mark told the principal only that Father Graff had exposed himself. The police were never called. "And from that point on, I just prayed to God that nobody would talk about it. I was humiliated. I didn't understand what the hell even happened. All I know is that, every night that I lay down to go to bed after that, all I did was think about it. Every single detail, over and over and over." In 1988, three years after the final assault, Father Graff was sent to a sexual abuse rehab clinic in New Mexico that had been set up by the Church. From there, he went to another diocese, where he continued to abuse children until he was finally arrested and put in jail. The priest later died in jail due to an accident.

Mark kept quiet about his experience that Saturday afternoon until March 26, 2009, when Artie, his second childhood friend abused by Father Graff, committed suicide. Mark entered a dark depression, barely able to get out of bed. He even contemplated suicide himself. His then wife saw what he was going through and told him, "You have a choice to make. You're either going to die or you're going to fight." So Mark went to the local newspaper to tell his story.

When his story was published in the local newspaper, he was amazed by the reaction: dozens of former students from his school came forward and admitted that they, too, had been similarly abused. "By the end of the third article, we had over forty kids just from my parochial school who had come forward to me with some type of abuse, whether from Father Graff or Father Shigo." He realized that, by coming out, he was not only helping himself heal, he was also helping others who had endured similar abuse. "For me, it was a healing process where I felt that I was worthy again. That I really could help people heal. I wasn't concerned about healing myself anymore. I put myself on the back burner." Seeing this reaction from his fellow classmates inspired Mark to call his representative in the Pennsylvania House of Representatives, Dante Santoni. He wanted to get involved in making a difference. Representative Santoni then scheduled an appointment for Mark with his colleague, Representative Tom Caltagirone, the Democratic chair of the Judiciary Committee at the time. Entering the representative's office, Mark saw pictures of popes and bishops hanging on the wall. He felt then that the conversation might not go well, and he was right. "I remember leaving and going down the elevator from his office. Representative Santoni was physically holding me up, with my wife on my other side. To hear that there was no chance—because the criminal statute of limitations had expired five years after the rape, and there was no recourse through the civil court, believing that nothing would ever be done—was just devastating."

The process of forgiveness took a long time. Mark can recall vividly the moment he forgave Father Graff for what he had done. "I can remember my daughter playing a lot of travel softball up and down the East Coast, and my sister had given me a book called *The Shack*." (*The Shack*, by William P. Young, is a novel about the abduction and murder of a young girl, and her father's struggles to understand her death.) "I was just struggling at the time. I can remember sitting in the outfield, by myself, and I just started bawling. I was like, 'You know what? I can forgive Father Graff.'" By releasing the anger he was carrying around, Mark was given a sense of hope that life could, in fact, get better. It was then that he allowed himself to move from a place of anger to a place of compassion for the priest. "I was hating God and hating religion and hating everything about the Church. I tried to take a step back and think about what happened to him. Maybe he was abused when he was young. Maybe he was abused in the Church, for all I know. He abused me, yes, but the only reason he was able to abuse me is because the bishops allowed this to happen." Mark looked at the full picture of the abuse that Graff had committed. Then he took the blame and anger that he had directed at the priest for so long and redirected it at the larger system that had allowed the abuse to take place. It was then that Mark decided to forgive. "I was like, 'You know what? I'm not going to hold this anger and pain.' I looked again at the bishops, the hierarchy at the Church, and that's where I diverted all my anger. Because they were the ones who allowed it to happen, and I will never forgive them for what they knew, for what they did." Still unable to forgive the higher-ups in the Catholic Church, Mark uses his anger as fuel for his fight for victims of sexual abuse.

The moment that Mark experienced on the field at his daughter's softball game was the moment of forgiveness that saved him. "I had no choice, because my family was suffering. We're driving and out of the blue I start bawling, and my daughter's wondering what's wrong with me. Why is Dad upset? I was going through so many problems and struggling, and it was eating me alive." After finishing the book his sister had given him, the forgiveness overflowed, not only for Father Graff, but also for the anger he had toward God. "God wasn't responsible for what happened to me. God is not the Church and the Church is not God. I don't know what this man's situation was. Maybe he got caught up in something and was never able to get away from it, and he ended up having problems." After his piece came out in the local paper, Mark remembers heading to church one morning when the monsignor stopped him and his family at the door, putting his arm across the entryway, and told them not to bother coming in. Since then, the only two times Mark has entered a Catholic church have been to bury two of his childhood friends, both of whom had been abused by Father Graff and later ended their own lives.

Releasing his anger toward Father Graff left Mark feeling lighter. "It was a huge weight off my shoulders, because I was so driven, trying to look for articles and trying to read everything I could, spending hours at night, reliving things in my head. It was just about letting it go. And understanding it wasn't my fault and I had nothing to do with it. It was all him." Being able to take his control back from Father Graff was the true act of forgiveness for Mark. "True forgiveness for me is, of course, not just words, but looking into my heart and having that feeling of being able to truly say, 'It's okay.' That whatever you did to me doesn't define me." He says the forgiveness was not just for his present self, but also for his younger self. He was finally able to set himself free. He was at last able to hold himself accountable for his own actions, and no longer blame his choices or his experiences in the present on the abuse he had suffered so long ago.

In 2011, Mark received a call from Representative Dante Santoni, who told him that he was planning on retiring, and he knew how important all the work was for Mark. The legislator told him that if he wanted an opportunity to enter politics, this would be the time. So Mark decided to run in the 2012 primary for Santoni's seat representing the 126th District in the Pennsylvania House of Representatives. During his campaign, Mark went door-to-door, trying to get people to support his campaign. "I would start telling my story, and I had so many people breaking down on the other side of that door. Women and men who would tell me for the first time what they'd never told anybody else. It was unbelievable. And even some of the men who wouldn't talk about it would be like, 'Please fight this. I'm not as strong as you. I can never talk about it, but you have my vote no matter what.'" Hearing that kind of feedback from his community fueled Mark in his fight. He learned that, in the state of Pennsylvania, "one in four girls and one in six boys will be sexually abused before the age of eighteen. And the worst part about it is, only one in nine will ever tell." Mark's campaign gained momentum, and he won the Democratic primary with close to 70 percent of the vote. He went on to win the general election in November 2012, and he was seated on January 1, 2013.

In 2016, Mark stood on the chamber floor of the Pennsylvania House of Representatives and made a heartfelt speech, pleading to his colleagues to support a bill that would eliminate the statute of limitations on childhood sex abuse cases. House representatives passed the bill with overwhelming support, and then sent it to the Senate, where the retroactive provision was stripped out, ultimately killing the bill. Similar legislation was again passed by the House in 2018, but as of this writing Republican senators continue to block the passage of the bill. At issue is the constitutionality of retroactively lifting the statute of limitations on childhood sex abuse crimes. Fortunately, there seems to be broad support for eliminating the statute of limitations for future child abuse victims.

For Mark, fighting for the rights of victims of sexual abuse will never be far from his mind. "It's almost part of my identity, and I think it is going to be a lifelong fight. It doesn't stop with this legislation. Even if we pass legislation, kids will continue to be abused. We need to have policies in place for those children, so that hopefully we have the right tools to help them heal at an earlier age and identify the abuser to prevent further abuse." Mark will never be able to erase the memories of the abuse he suffered, but he has found a way to forgive his abuser and restore his inner peace. And the anger that he still feels toward the Church continues to inspire his crusade to assure that no such abuse will ever be tolerated again.

I come from a large family of practicing Catholics. When the abuse stories came out in the news, I needed to take some time to process them and figure out how I felt about being a part of the Catholic Church moving forward. As a Catholic, and as a human being, I never want to be part of anything that condones the abuse of anyone, especially young children. The monsignor of the church I attend in Santa Monica addressed this issue in a sermon one day. He talked about the struggle to understand the reports coming out of so many churches, and he made it clear that neither he nor his parish tolerated any form of abuse. For me personally, when I think of being a part of the Catholic Church, I think specifically of my parish, the one that I grew up in, was baptized in, and attended and continue to attend. It is open, accepting, does great work for the community, and is a good place. That being said, even in good organizations terrible deeds can happen, and the perpetrators should be held accountable for their actions. I am hopeful that the Catholic Church will do better to change and grow, especially regarding topics like expanded roles for women, acceptance of divorce and homosexuality, and the elimination of abuse.

I knew that hearing Mark's story would be difficult. But I believe that those of us who are a part of the Catholic Church have a special duty to hear these stories, to bear witness to them so that they never happen again. Mark Rozzi is not an enemy of the Church—he is a crusader, and he deserves the gratitude and support of all those who believe in the sanctity of the Catholic faith.

Michelle LeClair

Breaking Free to Find Love

"Through forgiveness, you can quit suffering from
the sins committed against you."

—*Bryant McGill*

Michelle LeClair is a woman of great strength and resilience. As a teenager, she was in a near-fatal car accident that left her craving a spiritual presence in her life. She turned to her mother, who was an active member in the Church of Scientology. After meeting with a minister shortly after her accident, she became a dedicated member of the Church herself.

Early in her induction, Michelle attended a series of conversations with a Church-appointed mentor during which she was encouraged to talk openly about her life and would receive helpful guidance in return. This was one of the draws to Scientology: it seemed like an open and nurturing community. Michelle's mentor asked her about the people in her life and whether they, too, might be interested in joining the Church. If the answer was no, her mentor would advise her that she needed to change her social group and avoid people who didn't have the best interests of the Church in mind. It was during these sessions that Michelle first expressed her attraction to other women, thoughts that were quickly shut down by her mentor.

The founder of the Church of Scientology, L. Ron Hubbard, disapproved of homosexuality, stating that anyone with homosexual feelings should be considered "quite ill physically." He considered those who felt same-sex attraction "criminals," "evil," and "untrustworthy." As a consequence of confessing her true feelings, Michelle was required to approach members in the Church—most of whom she did not know—and "atone" for her lesbian thoughts and gather their signatures, all as a prerequisite to being accepted back into the Church. Although it was mortifying, Michelle did as she was told.

Desperate for acceptance within the Church, Michelle buried her same-sex feelings and married an aspiring actor whom she also convinced to join the Church. Her marriage quickly turned abusive after her husband discovered that the Church would always put the blame for any marital friction on Michelle. She attempted to get divorced within the first year, but wasn't successful. Instead, her husband would rely on the Church to reprimand Michelle for not "performing her wifely duties." Her husband quickly learned that, through humiliation, the use of the Church, and both mental and physical abuse, he could get what he wanted, and the abuse escalated over time. The Church suggested that the couple enlist in expensive Scientology marriage counseling. In these sessions, women were usually assigned the blame, and Michelle was frequently sent home with instructions to improve upon her role as a wife.

One enticement that the Church offered its members was the opportunity to work with business consultants. These consultants helped Michelle with her career and finances. In return, they encouraged her to share her wealth with the Church through donations. Soon, Michelle was running a highly successful insurance company. Publicly, she spoke highly of the Church, bringing in new converts and raising a small fortune. Over her years in the Church, she donated well over $5 million.

Despite the appearance of a wonderful life—financial success, four children, and a happy marriage—Michelle was privately miserable. She and her husband continued to go through marriage counseling. It was in these sessions that she again confessed her same-sex attraction and her desire to end her fourteen-year marriage. Divorce was discouraged, and the Church did not make the process easy. Finally, Michelle threatened to withhold any further donations. The following day, she was allowed to speak with a lawyer and draw up the divorce papers she had longed for.

Shortly after her divorce, Michelle met renowned music

producer Tena Clark. Their friendship quickly grew into a passionate relationship. After taking a trip together, Michelle received a call from her former mentor at the Church, asking if she was having an affair with a woman. At the time, she did not have the strength to admit she had fallen in love with Tena, even though she clearly had. It wasn't until 2010, after twenty-one years as a Scientologist, that Michelle finally gathered the courage to leave the Church and live freely with the woman she loved.

But quitting the Church of Scientology wasn't easy. Despite the stigma, Michelle managed to escape, along with her mother. As soon as she broke ties, she says the Church began to make her life a living hell. As she recounts, her phone and computer were hacked; she noticed suspicious cars parked outside her home; men in dark sunglasses followed her to the supermarket; and her kids were trailed to school. And this was only the beginning of her troubles.

One year after her departure from the Church, Michelle was charged by the state of California with running a Ponzi scheme, resulting in a legal battle that raged for many years. Ultimately, all criminal charges were dropped, but she had to pay several million dollars in legal fees, and still more to her clients who had lost money.

After such a grueling experience, it would seem that Michelle had a horde of people to forgive. But the person she had to forgive first and foremost was herself. She knew that she had played a role in the ordeal by allowing herself to be drawn into Scientology, by marrying a man she never loved, by investing in a businessman she never should have trusted—by letting herself be used by a group of people who groomed and coerced her through flattery and intimidation. They convinced her to follow their path and abandon her own. She had "put the ego ahead of the heart" and her personal ambition ahead of her conscience. She had placed more importance on her reputation than on the desires in her heart. She had made these mistakes as a young woman eager for approval and success. All of us have made mistakes in our youth—tempted into acts we later regretted—but very few of us have had to pay such a heavy price for our missteps. Forgiving herself was Michelle's path to redemption.

When I spoke to Michelle about her definition of forgiveness, she hesitated. And when I asked if she has been able to forgive the Church of Scientology for what she went through, she said, "If we can say that a definition of forgiveness could be to let go, then, yes, I would say that I was there. I don't think the act of saying 'I forgive you' means that what they did is somehow okay. I just have no emotion about it any longer, and I've let that go in my life 100 percent. Because that pain does not hurt anybody else but me, and my family, and my relationships." For Michelle, staying angry at the Church wouldn't change anything, so she did what was best for her and let her anger go.

But letting go is easier said than done, especially when you have ongoing struggles the way she does. That's why, for Michelle, forgiveness is like a "muscle that you have to build." The muscle may be weak at first, but over time it has the ability to grow stronger. One of the most important things she reminds herself is to always choose love over hate.

Often, we think we have done the work of forgiving, only to be faced with an incident that reminds us that there is more work to be done. At one point, Michelle realized that she hadn't truly forgiven herself the first time, so she needed to go back and do it again. As she says, "Instead of just kneeling and praying, this time I bowed as far down as my body could go. And I begged for forgiveness, and the words that came to me, the feeling that came to me was: 'I have forgiven you a long time ago. It is *you* who needs to forgive yourself.' I had this sensation wash over me of pure calmness—that my life had turned at just that moment."

Michelle had friends and family around her who helped her through the process of not only forgiving herself, but also releasing the negative feelings toward those involved. Those feelings didn't serve a purpose in her life any longer. "I can truly say that the resentment, the pain, the hate left me at that moment." For her, forgiveness has been a tool that has allowed her to shed the trauma of her past and leave herself open to the possibilities that lie ahead.

When I first interviewed Michelle, I thought she would focus on forgiving the Church for the harassment she'd endured. I was surprised to learn that her forgiveness was directed mostly toward herself. For me, her journey highlighted the importance of accepting responsibility for our own choices, even when they lead us into bitter hardships that are out of our control. Letting go did not mean that Michelle agreed with how she had been treated; rather, she recognized that she would never receive an apology from the Church of Scientology or be able to justify their behavior. In order to live her most authentic life, Michelle realized she had to be the one to dictate her own terms and find the courage to step away from the institution that was holding her back. I know I'll be keeping this lesson in mind—whether it pertains to an institution, a situation, a person, or anything else— as I seek to live my own most authentic life.

Sue Klebold

A Fallen Son

> "There is some good in the worst of us and some
> evil in the best of us. When we discover this, we
> are less prone to hate our enemies."
>
> —*Martin Luther King Jr.*

On April 20, 1999, two teenage boys, Eric Harris and Dylan Klebold, walked into Columbine High School in Littleton, Colorado, armed with high-powered weapons, and opened fire, murdering twelve students and a teacher and wounding more than twenty others. After exchanging gunfire with the police, both shooters took their own lives in the school library, leaving the world and their families in shock, with a host of unanswered questions. While their stated goal was to carry out a school bombing that would have rivaled the 1995 Oklahoma City bombing, the boys' motive for killing so many innocent people was unknown and remains a mystery to this day. Tragically, the Columbine shooting has acted as a blueprint for many mass shootings that have occurred since.

Dylan Klebold, who was said to have struggled with depression, wrote in his journal that the idea of killing himself gave him hope for a final escape from his dark thoughts. His mother, Sue Klebold, was unaware of her son's feelings. Dylan's final act showed Sue how little she had known about his inner turmoil. This horrific event left the town of Littleton and the rest of the world pointing blame at the boys' parents, asking what kind of people could let this happen. Sue was left with the same questions as she reflected on her role as a mother. She had always considered motherhood the most important role of her life, and one that she took great pride in. Suddenly, she felt as if she were on trial. "The whole world held us responsible. Our own governor went on national television to say this was the parents' fault." What the world didn't take into consideration was that, while Sue was enduring the hatred of the world, she was also grieving the loss of her son, whom she loved deeply.

Coping with the devastating loss of so many innocent people in addition to her son was, and still is, an agonizing process for Sue. From the moment she learned what her son had done, she questioned how it was possible for the boy she thought she knew so well to have committed such a heinous act. "I could not understand how Dylan could have been there that day. None of us who knew Dylan and loved him thought he was

ever capable of any kind of violence, because he just wasn't a
violent kid. He was a gentle, sort of pacifistic person. We
thought, 'Well, maybe this was some kind of a prank that had
gone wrong, or he's been brainwashed and he didn't intend to
be there.' We really believed things like that until we saw the
police report that came out six months later."

The immediate feelings of loss, confusion, and shock that
Sue experienced changed when she heard the police account of
the shooting. She had been in a state of denial. That shifted
when she gained some clarity on how those in her community,
and across the world, viewed her son. "I finally got to see the
person who everyone else saw, and that was the one moment
when I almost hated him. Up until that point, I was feeling
sympathetic, like something went wrong, he didn't intend to
be there, it wasn't planned, or it was some spontaneous thing.
I believed everything other than the truth, because I couldn't
wrap my arms around that. When I saw the sheriff's presenta-
tion and the tape the kids had made, and it was so full of pos-
turing and anger and loathing—they were just so horrible and
cold-blooded—that was the point I think I really felt anger at
Dylan. Because I could hear he was venting his anger against
the world, against people he knew, family members. He was so
overcome with disdain. I'd never seen anything like that."

Shocked by her son's overwhelming hatred and his eager-
ness to cut short so many innocent lives, Sue felt as if his actions were unforgivable. But ultimately, her role as his mother

allowed her to transcend her anger and seek a deeper under-standing of Dylan's struggles. "The mother's love for him just completely obliterated any anger I had. I couldn't sustain anger when I had a broken heart and was missing him so much. Sometimes people hate their loved ones who perpetrate vio-lence, and blame them for years. That wasn't my personal ex-perience. My experience was concluding that he had to be in some horrible place to become the person that I saw, and it was my job as his mother to try to figure out how he got there—what that place was."

Sue learned that her son had been struggling with thoughts of suicide. It was "his own mind, his own distortion, his own suffering that put him in that place." Learning how much pain he was suffering allowed her to let go of her anger while seek-ing answers. "I can't use the word 'forgive'—I think the word that I would use is 'understand.' As soon as we try to under-stand why someone has done what they've done, the need for forgiveness just goes out the window. If you have empathy, there is no need to forgive, because you understand, you're walking in their shoes, you have their frame of mind, and that feeling of blame just goes away." Sue tries to be kind to herself, to not blame herself for not being aware of her son's demons, but it is something she cannot fully resolve. "I know that I raised him to have love and morality and respect for his fellow man. I did everything I knew to instill those things, so I don't feel that I put that kind of hatred in him." Knowing that she did all she could to raise a loving human being has helped her to manage her sorrow and humiliation.

Sue's situation and her relationship to the concept of forgiveness may be difficult for others to understand. While many people may instinctively feel anger toward the parents of a school shooter—blaming them for their child's actions—she explains that anger and forgiveness are equally hard for her to accept from others. "One thing that's always been difficult for me is when someone says, 'I forgive you.' That makes me feel defensive, because I wonder, 'What are you forgiving me for?' I was the best mother I knew how to be. I didn't know what my child was going through. I would have done anything in the world to prevent what happened if I had known. Forgiveness can carry a kind of superiority, or condescension, or even self-righteousness. When we talk about forgiving others, we have to be mindful that forgiving somebody else puts us in a position where we in some way are feeling superior to another human being. We are saying, 'I forgive you,' as if we are bestowing on them some great gift that they should be worthy of."

It has been challenging for Sue to have so many people offer her forgiveness. "I don't want to be forgiven, because that implies that I've done something wrong for which I need to be forgiven. What Dylan did was unforgivable. My own work with forgiveness centers around my relationship with him. If I would ever come face-to-face with Dylan again, the first thing

I would say to him is: 'Can you forgive me? Can you forgive me for not being the kind of person who you could trust? For not being knowledgeable enough to know that you were suffering, to know the right words to say, to know how to help you?' That is where my struggle has been, and I've come to the conclusion that as a mother who's lost a child to suicide, we can never fully forgive ourselves."

Sue knows that she will never get over her son's suicide, and she is left with the conviction that his is the only forgiveness that would truly matter to her. In his absence, she is left with feelings of guilt and sadness that she was unable to be a better mother to her son, who so desperately needed help. "I don't know of a single parent or loved one of someone who died from suicide who completely forgives themselves. In our minds, that person chose to leave us. Even when we tried our best and they were in treatment . . . and Dylan was not. He didn't have any kind of diagnosis. The hard, hard work is forgiving ourselves." When someone approaches Sue to forgive her, she reminds herself, "Forgiveness is a gift we give to ourselves. If others are able to give themselves the gift of forgiving me, it's really not about me at all—it's about them. And that's a good thing for them. I understand that need completely."

Sue has struggled to live without her son. "I've come to the conclusion that I will never really forgive myself. And that's okay, because why should I beat myself up for not forgiving myself? I have plenty of other things to beat myself up for. I accept that forgiving myself is probably the one thing I'll never fully be able to do. But what I've done with that feeling is that I've tried to turn it into action." Sue lives every day in memory of her son Dylan, trying to spread awareness and help other parents who might be in a similar situation, in the hopes of guiding them toward a healthy resolution. "I try to live my life dedicated to Dylan's memory, and try to think what might have helped him. That's why I talk to people. I talk to parents, and I talk to teachers, and school personnel, and law enforcement, and say, 'There are some things we've got to understand about people who are suffering, and in Dylan's case, people who are enraged and suffering simultaneously. That can make them dangerous.'" The fact that Sue was unable to detect her son's depression and give him the help he needed will always haunt her.

When it comes to living a life free from anger, Sue is quick to say that she has never been the type to carry anger, and does not consider herself an angry person now. While she is clear that she has left any negative feelings behind her, she doesn't want to live without the memory of her son. Preserving his memory is important to her. "I don't want freedom from him. I don't ever want to put this down, because it's what keeps me close to Dylan." It is the idea that she or someone might have been able to prevent her son from taking his own life and the lives of so many others that leaves Sue wanting to share her knowledge. "What I feel inside is this ache in my heart because

I believe that tragedies such as this can be prevented. I really believe that suicide can be prevented if we have the right tools and resources and do and say the right things when someone is in crisis. I didn't have the knowledge, but if I had, it might have changed what happened. But it's that feeling of knowing that I might have helped someone and didn't that has made me put those feelings into action and say to myself, 'Share the tools. Tell people what you wish you'd known. Tell them what you wish you'd said.'"

Sue hopes that her message will reach the countless people who have been touched by suicide and that it will help others avoid the losses that she and her community have suffered. "Trying to help others is my way of sending love to all those who were killed and injured, every minute of every day." It is the memory of her son that allows her to spread awareness and educate those who may be in a similar situation to hers. She hopes that, somewhere, Dylan is feeling the love that his mother has for him—a love that shows in all the work she does in his memory. "I will never really forgive myself, because I never want to let myself forget that there were things I could have done. I don't want anyone to forget that we must never stop trying to help. If there are any hidden gifts to be found in all the years of sorrow, perhaps it's greater empathy for mankind and deeper understanding of the many ways that life can be painful."

While Sue is uncomfortable with the idea of others forgiving her, she is also very clear that if she had been in the shoes of a family whose child was killed, she would feel the same way toward her that some of them do. "I know in my heart that if it had been the other way around and my son had been killed by one of their children, I'm certain that I would have felt anger and judgment." One of her struggles has been with the blame the governor and the nation put on her after the shooting. "Assigning blame never promotes healing. Ever. So it was hard for me to accept and forgive that. But it was that level of blame that sparked in me a need to educate, because if people were ignorant enough to believe in such a simple explanation, it was my call to action. It made me stand up and say, 'Wait a minute—this isn't why this happened. And if people believe that this is the reason, they're putting themselves in greater danger.' I don't like ignorance, and I want to do everything I can to eradicate it."

Sue has had time and distance from the mass of people who blamed her for the Columbine shooting. While she doesn't believe in the concept of forgiving those who put the blame for her son's actions on her, she knows that being resentful is a waste of her energy. "I don't forgive people. I don't need to forgive people. I think the whole concept of forgiving people is egocentric and egotistical. This is why this discussion is so difficult to have—because I understand that my forgiving someone else isn't about my relationship with that person. It's about my relationship with myself. I am willing to let go of anger, because letting go of that anger is going to make me feel happier. That's really what the whole discussion of forgiveness is about. It's not between you and that person—it's between you and yourself." Instead of using the word "forgiveness," Sue prefers to focus on other words, such as "balance," "integration," "recovery," and "empathy." She believes that all of us on earth are equal, and that the act of telling someone that you forgive them creates an inequality, giving the forgiver the upper hand.

Twenty years after the Columbine shooting—twenty years after losing her son—the hardest thing for Sue is working on forgiving herself. "I still think our hardest task is forgiving ourselves. I will never stop accepting the responsibility that there were things I could have done to prevent this terrible tragedy, if I had only known what those things were." She will always regret not knowing how desperate her son had become, and she will always carry the burden of wondering if she could've done more had she been aware of her son's pain. Before Dylan took his own life, Sue had never thought much about forgiveness. Though this tragedy has given her a much more profound understanding of the process, it has not shaken her conviction that forgiving someone is a gift you can only give to yourself. "I think I took a deeper dive into what forgiveness means, but I don't think that dive changed how I feel about it."

I am sure some people who read Sue's story will have conflicting feelings about her views on forgiveness. Some may read this and feel they can relate, while others won't, and that's okay. When we hear horrible stories like this one, we don't usually think of how challenging it might be for the family of the person who caused so much pain. Instead, we think of the victims whose lives were taken and their families, who were suddenly left with a new reality. It's difficult to imagine the sort of suffering Sue has experienced in the past twenty years. Like so many parents who lost children on that tragic day, she is left with a terrible emptiness—a hole where so much love and hope for the future had been stored. But while other parents received sympathy, Sue received anger. I can see how the forgiveness of others might seem like cold comfort to a mother forced to carry a double burden of grief and guilt—grief for a child she loved so dearly, and guilt over never knowing his pain and not being able to reach him and help him in time.

Sue's view of forgiveness was one I had never heard before. At first, I wasn't able to relate to her perspective. For her, saying "I forgive you" feels like a declaration loaded with condescension, which now I can understand. I don't have the same reaction to hearing those words, so my own experience of forgiveness is different. But my conversation with Sue further proved to me how complex and layered the topic of forgiveness truly is. What forgiveness means to me could be something completely different from what it is for you—and that's okay. It is only with open and honest conversation, and compassion, that we will deepen our understanding of forgiveness and adapt our behavior accordingly for our own growth.

All profits that Sue Klebold has earned from her book, A Mother's Reckoning, *have been donated to mental health organizations and to support research into suicide prevention.*

Talinda Bennington

A Vanished Love

"Therefore we must be saved by the final form of
love which is forgiveness."

—*Reinhold Niebuhr*

On July 20, 2017, musician Chester Bennington, of Linkin
Park, was found dead in his home in Palos Verdes, California, the victim of suicide. His wife of twelve years, Talinda,
her three kids with Chester, and her three stepchildren all
mourned the loss and wondered what they could've done to
prevent the tragedy. Losing a loved one to suicide leaves survivors with a cauldron of different emotions. Talinda says, "Forgiveness was one of my first feelings, the first emotion that I
truly identified with, because I knew he was not well." She had
been well acquainted with her husband's struggle with depression, and she'd tried to help him get ahold of his demons. She
was there during all of his ups and downs. "I knew he didn't
ever intend to hurt any of us. My gut feeling was he was in a

dark place and he just didn't get out of it this time—it wasn't his first attempt." Talinda was able to empathize with her husband's depression and suicide because she had witnessed his long struggle to control his illness. He had been attending outpatient therapy for more than six months before his death, actively working on his sobriety and depression. "We thought he was okay; he was at the top of his game. He had a number one album. He was speaking a lot about these deep, dark thoughts, which is a step in recovery, so they thought it was okay."

Chester had been coping with depression and addiction his entire life. Behind his public persona, Talinda had watched and loved her husband throughout his private battle, which is why she felt such compassion and sadness after his suicide. Her personal feelings were in stark contrast to the public bashing she had to endure from some of Chester's fans, who blamed her for her husband's death. Some took to social media to blame her for not being more attentive to his mental health struggle. The backlash left her feeling wounded and resentful toward her husband's choice to end his life, forcing her to carry this painful burden alone. She recalls moments when she would ask, "How dare you leave me with all of this to handle." After six months of coping with the ongoing attacks, she finally accepted that she couldn't control what was being said about her, or the pain and frustration that others were feeling over her husband's death. "When somebody loses somebody they love, whether they know them or not, they just want to blame somebody. And I'm the easiest person to blame." It was with this realization that she felt she had truly arrived at a place of forgiveness.

For Talinda, forgiveness is a process that she comes face-to-face with on a daily basis. To help her cope with the loss of her husband, and to continue his legacy, she now travels around the country speaking about suicide prevention and mental health awareness. She shares her story, knowing that she will get backlash, in the hopes of helping others who may be suffering as she and Chester suffered. She wants to give hope to others who might be struggling the way her husband was and guide them to a better outcome. It hasn't been easy for her to face the hatred on such a frequent basis. When she encounters it, she tries to remember that the hate being expressed is coming from a place of pain, hurt, and loss. She reminds herself that she, too, has to forgive and move on. She draws strength from the knowledge that she has to be a positive role model for her children, who are also dealing with the new reality of life without their father. She reminds them to "stay with your truth" and not to pay attention to the negativity.

Being present for her children while also managing her grief continues to pose challenges for Talinda. Sometimes she questions how her husband could have left her with this harsh new reality. "Not only do I have to deal with our children crying and grieving, I have to deal with this publicly. I have to monitor my social media accounts and remove the hate that's on there, because there are hundreds of people looking at that for inspiration and help, and I can't have that out there. So I get really angry with that, and that gets directed toward him. But I quickly realized it's not him." What continues to anger Talinda is the suffering of their children. "I do get angry for them. It makes me very sad, because they deserve a father. To have to look your kids in the eye and say, 'Dad's gone,' is something I wouldn't wish on my worst enemy. That came with a lot of anger. And I had to forgive, because if I hold on to that anger, then I can't love my kids with an open heart and help them through their pain."

One of the most important steps Talinda had to take in forgiving herself was recognizing that there was nothing she or anyone else could have done to save her husband. He was "just not well, and he made a tragic mistake." She recalls all the times Chester had been open with her about his struggle with depression, and how he felt that his family would be better off without him. "I try to remember that it was that broken part of him that took that action that night. And I can't help but forgive him, because he truly loved us. He truly loved me. He was such a great dad. He was just not well, and he was so good at hiding it that it makes me almost have even more compassion for him, because that's a lot of work. It's a lot of work to feel that bad and to not let anybody know."

The last moments Talinda shared with Chester before his

death had made it seem like he was in a stable place. When she reflects on the days leading up to his death, she wishes she had been more aware of his internal struggles, but she also knows that her help was often met with anger and denial. In the past, when she had tried to offer him the tools he needed to get to a better place, he resented her and pushed her away. It was the unwell part of Chester that isolated himself, rather than alerting her to his depression. Over the years she spent with her husband, she'd become familiar with the signs of addiction, but the signs of depression were much harder to recognize. "Depression doesn't have a face, and it could look like somebody's fully happy," she explains. She knew that while she loved her husband and desperately wanted to get him the help he needed, it was ultimately in Chester's hands to help himself.

Talinda will never know if Chester truly meant to end his life that night, but learning to cope openly with the pain, especially for her children, is her main focus today. She wants her kids to know that they are not alone in grieving the loss of their father, and that everything they are experiencing is okay. But there are times when her grief as a wife conflicts with her grief as a mother. "I feel like my marriage was betrayed, because he left. He left. He chose not to be here. And that's betrayal, and with that definitely has to come some sort of forgiveness. But I feel that forgiveness when I understand his illness and his state of mind of thinking that we'd be better off without him, which is so not true." Remembering that it was the mentally ill part of her husband that drove him to end his life allows her to let go of her anger and forgive him for his suicide. Talinda knows that she has the choice to forgive or to resent, and she has chosen to forgive.

Since the death of her husband, Talinda's definition of forgiveness has become more solidified than ever before. The core is acceptance, which allows her to release her anger. Now, whenever she feels hurt, she also tries to look at her own actions to identify any role she may have played. If she notices that she has contributed negatively to a situation, she asks for forgiveness. But she knows that, in the end, forgiveness is something you do for yourself.

We all know someone who has struggled with mental health issues. It's one of the most baffling challenges—almost like fighting a ghost: it can appear suddenly, then vanish, constantly changing shape. When you think it's finally gone, it can return, darker than ever. And its greatest victim can seem like its most loyal ally, hiding symptoms and reassuring us when we should be most concerned. Talinda's openness about Chester's depression and death aims to lessen the stigma and bring much-needed attention to a crisis that cuts across every part of our society.

For me, hearing others' experiences with the struggle to forgive—whether in dealing with loss or managing a changing relationship—has informed my own understanding of forgiveness and has pushed me to be more open about my own experiences. Listening to Talinda's journey highlights the challenge of finding forgiveness when the person you need to forgive is no longer here to talk it through. Her courage showed me that, when that happens, increasing the dialogue about mental health is the only way forward, to let those in pain know that there are other options on how to ease their suffering.

Mark Kelly

A Newfound Mission

"His heart was as great as the world, but there was
no room in it to hold the memory of a wrong."

—*Ralph Waldo Emerson*

On January 8, 2011, U.S. Representative Gabby Giffords
was outside a Safeway supermarket speaking to constituents in an event she called "Congress on Your Corner." It was
typical of the Arizona congresswoman to reach out directly
to the people of her district, learning about the issues that
mattered most to them. Within the crowd was a young man
named Jared Loughner. Without warning, he drew a handgun
and shot Representative Giffords through the head. Then he
turned his gun on the rest of the crowd. The shooting rampage
took the lives of six and left another thirteen injured. Giffords's husband, Mark Kelly, was in the middle of his training
for his last space shuttle flight when he was informed of the

assassination attempt on his wife. He immediately rushed to her side.

As the commander of the final flight of the space shuttle *Endeavour*, Mark had been trained to manage stressful missions with high stakes. He was now focused on the survival and recovery of his wife. His new mission allowed him little time to dwell on the man who had caused this tragedy. "I didn't have time to be incredibly bitter about this individual. It would've been a big time suck, which was the last thing I needed. I just had to focus on, 'What do I need to do right now to help Gabby and deal with this situation?'" Mark is aware that his reaction was unusual. From the first instant, he treated the shooting as an event in the past and kept his attention locked on his wife's immediate needs and future recovery. He never shied from the task at hand, and he never let anger drain his energy. "The individual who did this was almost a nonfactor. At this point, he doesn't matter. Absent of creating a time machine, you're not gonna fix this problem. It's not gonna go away." He ignored Loughner and focused instead on his wife. "Jared Loughner was somebody else's problem. That was the problem of the United States Attorney and the FBI at that point. That's their thing to worry about. I didn't even think about it." Mark's ability to see the shooter as irrelevant to the mission at hand—Gabby's recovery—shows his remarkable discipline.

Eight years after the attack, Mark is still fully dedicated to his wife's recovery. He told me that he never experienced any stages in the path toward forgiveness. His focus has always been on his wife; he doesn't let himself become distracted by feelings toward Loughner. The shooting is in the past, and carrying any negativity forward would take away from the positivity needed to ensure his wife's healing. "I didn't have the time to deal with it. I just was kind of like, 'Move on.'"

Once Gabby was released from the hospital, she needed to decide whether she would continue with her career in Congress. In the early days of 2012, Gabby reluctantly accepted that she was no longer able to serve her constituents as she had in the past, and so she resigned. Although she was out of the hospital, she was still going in for care every day for another six months, meeting with various doctors. As a new sense of normalcy emerged, Mark was finally able to take a breath. After his wife's resignation in January 2012, Mark recalls a feeling of relief, unclouded by thoughts of revenge. "It just felt like a new dawn. When you ask about forgiveness—if I had forgiven this guy—it never came up. It was never something that I considered was important, necessary, something I needed to do because I'd just moved on. He's in jail. Never gonna hear from him again."

If Mark's single-minded focus on his wife's recovery kept him from having thoughts of rage and revenge, it has also kept him from having thoughts of forgiveness. "If you would've asked me if I'd forgiven him, I would say: I don't even consider that as a thing. For me, it doesn't matter. I didn't have time." Mark's ability to control his thoughts may seem almost super-human, but he remains deeply empathetic, even toward his wife's attacker. When Mark considers Loughner's motivations, he says, "He was mentally ill, which, for me, is a factor here." Instead of fixating on his wife's attacker, he directs his frustra-tion at the system for failing a young man who so clearly needed help. Mark feels that if Jared had been given the proper care for his mental illness, the tragedy might have been avoided. Still, thoughts of resentment and revenge don't come easily to Mark, and so he doesn't feel the same need that so many of us have to untangle our emotions after a trauma.

For many of us, the act of forgiveness is a necessary step in order to move beyond a traumatic incident; it allows us to re-lease any anger that might be holding us back, tying us to the pain, and trapping us in our darkest moments. For Mark, this process came quickly and naturally, through an act of will: "I don't allow myself to be angry. Because not only did this indi-vidual do this and forever change Gabby's life and the lives of the six people killed and thirteen injured, but in a sense he is also continuing to have an effect on me—and I won't allow that to happen." Mark recognizes that holding on to anger would only distract him from the needs of his wife. Like her husband, Gabby does not hold resentment toward the man who shot her. It's in the character of both Mark and Gabby to be forgiving people, but it's also a deliberate choice.

As the years have passed, Mark has stayed true to his mission. He tries to focus his energy on the present, rather than on a past he is unable to change. He has never let the shooting take away from the love and joy he shares with his wife. Since then, he and Gabby have focused their attention on making sure something like this does not happen again. They have worked hard to raise money and awareness to pass stronger gun laws. In fact, Mark is now running for the Senate in Arizona to enact further change. "We're trying to take this horrible thing that happened to Gabby and turn it into some lives saved, especially little kids."

Mark was able to shed the past much faster than most of us would be able to should we find ourselves in a similar situation. Though it's important to go at your own pace, what I took away from his experience is that, sometimes, refocusing your energy can be a positive way forward, ensuring that you don't stay stuck in an event from the past. Instead of grappling with anger and resentment, he focused his thoughts on the task at hand: helping his wife recover. I think most of us, myself included, would say that it's easier said than done, but Mark's is a method of coping that we can certainly admire and aspire to.

I'm sure we would all like to be able to follow in Mark's footsteps by training our minds to focus on the positive things we can do in the wake of a tragedy—I know I would. Even if I should stumble at times, it will always inspire me to know that people like Mark have worked toward recovery—directing their energy away from a past they cannot change and toward a more hopeful future for us all.

Iskra Lawrence

Embracing Beauty

> "Life, that ever needs forgiveness, has, for its first
> duty, to forgive."
>
> —*Edward Bulwer-Lytton*

The journey to find self-love wasn't an easy one for Iskra Lawrence. Bombarded by ideals of beauty throughout her childhood—from movies to billboards—she absorbed a distorted image of how she should look and act in order to one day grace the pages of glamour magazines. At thirteen, she entered the world of modeling by way of an *Elle*-sponsored competition for young supermodels. As she navigated the dizzying world of agencies and photo shoots, she was given a hard lesson in the math of modeling: "Your hips should be thirty-four inches, your waist should be twenty-four inches, you need to be at least five-nine, with clear skin and smooth, healthy hair and straight white teeth." She also recalls being given a rating on a scale of one to ten by the modeling agencies. Iskra took this number to heart. She says she "saw it as competing against myself and this ideal." Whatever the agencies told her she needed to have, she wanted it.

Iskra recalls going to any length necessary in order to achieve what these agencies were searching for. As a teenager, she turned to magazines to guide her in her pursuit of perfection. She tried all the fad diets touted by celebrities. Little by little, she internalized the unnatural ideals that were asked of her. "You get addicted to that feeling of measuring yourself, seeing the results, because you're essentially starving yourself, restricting yourself, or exercising to the point of exhaustion. And you just wanted to see more results; you wanted to get closer to that goal." As she immersed herself in the modeling world, her perspective became completely distorted. As she says, "This desire to be slim and to attain this perfected beauty ideal consumed me—consumed my thoughts, my passions, my drives." Each morning, she looked in the mirror and hated what she saw. "I would hold parts of my body that had the most fat on them—I would grab them and want them to disappear. I'd google operations that would make my calves smaller." Iskra was being smothered by self-loathing: "Layers and layers of hatred and disgust for your own body, wishing you could just cut chunks off your body just to get smaller."

Finally, her self-loathing reached a breaking point. She realized that by continuing this destructive behavior, she was disrespecting the body that God had created and "that isn't meant to be perfect." It was at this point that she discovered plus-size modeling. Ironically, after visiting an agency specifically catering to plus-size models, Iskra was told that she was too small. She was left wondering if she would ever be able to fit anyone's ideals of true beauty. She was forced to reexamine her relationship to the modeling world—forced to ask herself whether "all this effort, all this time, all this sacrifice, all this pain and hate and hurt has really been for nothing. I'm just losing this battle and not living my life and not being happy—every single day just investing time into this fruitless mission to try to change this body into something it can't be and it's not meant to be." She questioned why the modeling agency drove people to hate themselves, rather than highlighting the unique beauty within. Iskra was determined to prove that there are a variety of ways "to model, to have a body, to feel beautiful and portray different types of beauty in this world." This quickly became her mission: "I switched from changing myself and my body to trying to change the industry."

Iskra shifted her ambition away from impossible standards and toward becoming the best version of herself—but it wasn't easy. "In my head, I thought, 'I will never be on the cover of *Vogue* or in these editorials and be the face of a beautiful fragrance campaign.' I had to rethink all of my dreams and goals, and realize that actually maybe I can just be the model that I want to see." She realized that perhaps she had gone through all the body image struggle for a reason; perhaps God had a calling for her that was much bigger than she ever knew. She decided to take ownership of her struggle and use her experience of feeling "less than" to help others who might be in a similar place.

Iskra began by talking to her friends, openly and honestly, sharing her journey and letting them know that they were not alone. Then she expanded the conversation through social media channels, reaching a far wider audience than she'd ever dreamed of reaching before. She spoke candidly about her eating disorder, her insecurities, and her challenges with body dysmorphia. By baring her insecurities online to people all over the world, Iskra began her journey of healing and forgiveness.

At first, Iskra felt a need to forgive her body for the pain it had caused her. But she soon realized that she really needed to forgive herself for "allowing that power to overtake my life and to have this control." She had to forgive herself for letting her eating disorder and body dysmorphia consume so much of her life. She had to become aware that, while those struggles were a part of her story, they did not define her. This first step was the hardest—"forgiving myself, because part of me sees other people who didn't waste that time." She had to confront the fact that she had allowed herself to fall victim to unhealthy standards and that she had tortured her body to suit the tastes of others. "I had to forgive myself. I was young. I was essentially mentally ill, with an eating disorder and body dysmorphia, and was struggling with the whole thing by myself in secret. So that definitely was a huge part of forgiveness."

As part of Iskra's journey of forgiveness, she created a practice she calls the "mirror challenge": "Getting in front of the mirror and looking at my body and telling my body, 'I love you.' And instead of seeing the things that I before saw through the lens of self-hatred, looking at my body and finding out why I appreciate it and why I value it and why I should be celebrating it. Yes, my thighs are bigger, but that means they're super strong and that means I can jump really high." This act of looking in the mirror, picking out parts of her body that she'd once viewed as flawed and instead celebrating them, was a big step in learning to forgive herself and showing her body the love that she had been withholding. "Your skin, your body—all of you deserves loving language." After years of self-criticism, Iskra has made this mirror practice a daily ritual, and it's become a vital part of her journey.

There are still times when negative self-talk creeps back into Iskra's thoughts. On those days, she reminds herself of all the things she has to be grateful for. "Gratitude is huge," she says. She practices gratitude in front of the mirror and by leaving little notes to herself that she'll rediscover throughout the day. Part of her process of forgiving is the awareness that there will be times when the negative self-talk returns, and she must forgive herself in those moments as well. "We have to be very forgiving for all of the emotions that we feel and the thoughts that we let enter our minds—be forgiving with that. Be gentle, be accepting." It's important to be realistic, to be aware that you will have great days and you will have bad days. Forgiveness allows Iskra to get past the bad days and move forward in a place of love.

Through her journey, Iskra has developed a mantra that puts her mind, body, and spirit in a place of love and acceptance. "The thing that instills deep confidence in myself is the phrase 'I am enough.' I use it in everyday scenarios, in every single part of my life—with relationships or at work—just knowing *I am enough*." This beautiful phrase marks her triumph over the doubts and uncertainties that plagued her. It is an affirmation of her worth and an acceptance of her self. It is Iskra's realization that "I deserve my own love and kindness, and anything that I decided to do or have done is okay, and was meant to be. I value everything that I've been through, and I use that to be the best possible person I can be every single day when I wake up."

Many of us share the struggle to forgive ourselves for the shame we feel toward our bodies. Growing up in Los Angeles, I remember—from a very young age—feeling pressure to look like someone I wasn't. I remember trying to keep myself under a certain weight, not liking my curves when I went through puberty, feeling like I didn't know my own body when I gained weight in high school. I tortured myself by criticizing my body through the ups and downs of an unhealthy relationship, trying every fad diet I could find, taking diuretics and diet pills, and always talking about my body in a negative way to my girlfriends. I remember holding my body to impossible standards and not appreciating it for all its ability and health.

I, like many other women, can relate to Iskra's journey from resenting your body to embracing it. As she mentioned, forgiving our bodies and ourselves is an ongoing practice. But making the decision to speak to your body in a kind and loving way—and thanking your body for its strength, health, and abilities—is a decision you can make any day.

Accepting our bodies is one of the greatest gifts we can give ourselves. Loving ourselves despite inevitable changes isn't easy, but Iskra reminds me that having a practice—like her mirror ritual—is a great way to stay on track and to begin each day in a place of forgiveness, love, and acceptance for the bodies we have been given.

Tanya Brown

Hope for My Sister

> "Forgiveness is not always easy. At times it feels more painful than the wound we suffered, to forgive the one who inflicted it. And yet there is no peace without forgiveness."
>
> —*Marianne Williamson*

On June 12, 1994, Nicole Brown Simpson was brutally murdered at her home in Brentwood, California. Her sister, Tanya Brown, was twenty-four years old at the time. For the next eleven months, Nicole's ex-husband, O. J. Simpson, stood trial for her murder, dragging the Brown family through a very public proceeding, often called "the trial of the century." Finally, on October 3, 1995, O. J. Simpson was found not guilty—a verdict that provided very little closure for the mourning family. Because of the media frenzy surrounding the event, Tanya was not able to process her grief for many years. This unresolved trauma took a terrible toll—emotionally and physically. Her journey toward acceptance serves as a poignant testament to the power of forgiveness.

Nicole's murder affected each member of the Brown family differently, and they all processed the loss in their own ways. The family's immediate concern was for the two children Nicole and O.J. had shared. Tanya's parents immediately forgave O.J. in order to give all of their attention to the kids and to allow themselves to move on from the loss of their daughter. As Tanya told me, "They forgave the action so they could move on." The children helped sustain the family. Tanya remembers that they were the "biggest gifts we could have had, because they kept us busy. We kept them busy." Her parents felt dragging the pain forward would only cause the children more harm. According to Tanya, their attitude became "We've got to let it go. It is what it is. We need to move forward." Trying to create a normal life for the two kids was what helped the Brown family move forward. But Tanya's grieving process had barely begun.

Tanya could not begin her journey toward acceptance until she had uncovered the truth about her sister's death. For almost two years after the murder, she did not believe that O.J. was responsible. She could not imagine that the man who had sworn to love and protect her sister would have cut her down. It wasn't until the DNA evidence was revealed in the courtroom that Tanya felt confident that O.J. was guilty. Knowing the circumstances of her sister's death was a vital step in her struggle to accept it and move on. But this struggle would take over a decade, and it required extraordinary faith.

The Browns had never been a very religious family, but Tanya recalls a spiritually defining moment that occurred shortly after Nicole's death. She remembers a shrine in her family home dedicated to her sister, where her family received hundreds of letters and prayers from people all over the world. One night, she found her mother sitting at the shrine with a pained look on her face. Tanya asked her what was wrong. Her mother said that while she was grateful for all the prayers and blessings, they made her realize that she and her family weren't very religious. Tanya quickly responded that her family might not attend church regularly, but they had deep faith: "We believe. We have faith. We know where Nicole is. We believe in afterlife. Everything will be okay." This moment with her mother reassured Tanya that she wasn't going through this journey alone—they were all grieving the loss together, as a family.

About two years after Nicole's murder, Tanya found herself sitting in a church with her family, asking for a way to move on. She had watched both her mother and father accept the loss of their daughter in a way she wanted to emulate, but forgiving wasn't easy for her. She marveled at her mother's strength: "She doesn't forget, but she forgives. She doesn't allow things to manifest in an ugly way." Tanya knew this was the path forward. But she still couldn't shed the pain, so she turned to God for help. She recalls saying, "God, take away this pain. Help me move on." And she remembers—sitting in that church with her family around her—feeling a sense of light she hadn't felt before. But, still, she was unable to release her pain, and darker days lay ahead.

Ten years after her sister's murder, overwhelmed by her unresolved grief, Tanya attempted suicide. This would prove to be the turning point. It was in the treatment center that she learned about the power of forgiveness: "I learned acceptance. I learned how to surrender to pain. I learned how to accept loss. I learned how to really move forward. It wasn't just Nicole. It was a culmination of pain I'd suffered throughout my life, and it caught up with me, because I didn't face my trauma, tragedy, and losses."

In treatment, Tanya began a personal rebirth that has enhanced every aspect of her life. "I learned self-love, self-respect, self-forgiveness, giving yourself grace." She finally had the time and space to process the pain she had been carrying for years. She was finally able to feel, cry, and journal about her emotions—a new habit that proved indispensable: "If somebody does you harm, take a pen to paper and write about it." In therapy she also discovered the Serenity Prayer: "God, grant me the serenity to accept the things I cannot change, the courage to change the things I can, and the wisdom to know the difference." Surrounded by others who were grappling with their own burdens of grief, Tanya began praying to God to see them all through their challenging times. In treatment she learned that you can't get through the hard times alone. So she turned to God and had faith that, no matter how challenging life might become, prayer and belief would get her through.

Tanya knows that everyone's journey toward forgiveness is different, and some never get to that place. When I asked her if she had forgiven O. J. Simpson, she said she has moved on and does not carry anger toward him. "I have no interest in the guy—he just doesn't matter. I don't wish him ill. I don't wish him death. I don't wish him pain, because there are two children we need to think about." Having her niece and nephew to care for has helped Tanya in her healing process. To be fully present with them, she has learned to release any negative feelings she has toward their father and make sure that he has no presence in her life. For Tanya, that is what forgiveness is: "Giving yourself permission to say, 'You are not going to control me.'" Her sister's death will always be a part of her story, but she has learned that it doesn't define who she is. "Nicole, O.J., all of that—it used to be my identity when I was twenty-four, because we kind of got thrust into this circus. But as years passed—no, this is not my identity. It's just something I went through."

Tanya's journey toward forgiveness unfolded in its own time. Today, she tries to remain fully present in each moment, processing life's experiences as they come. She also tries to help her sisters in their paths toward letting go, knowing that there is "no timetable on when you're ready" to get to a place of forgiveness. For Tanya, "forgiveness is not about releasing the person who hurt you from their responsibility; it's about releasing yourself from the trauma."

Tanya also refers to the teachings of the comedian and author Russell Brand. She credits Brand with teaching her about getting to a place of acceptance and forgiveness. "He says, 'We all have a hole in the soul, and we try to feed it with something. And that something can be positive, or that something can be destructive.'" It's up to each of us to choose a healthy course, center ourselves, and put ourselves on a path toward releasing our pain and arriving at a place of forgiveness.

After completing her treatment, Tanya has been able to reclaim her life. Today, she shares the lessons she has learned with others as a life coach. She teaches others that chaos and stress will come and go, but by remaining centered and in a place of self-love, you can remain in control of your journey. She serves as an example of the message she spreads: "To take the wrongdoing that somebody has done to you and make it a positive to help yourself and to help other people." Tanya is able to reflect on the loss of her sister Nicole, and though she still misses and thinks often of her, she has been able to move on; she doesn't allow it to occupy space in her life. She has also written a book on her journey in order to share her insights with others. She hopes that being open and honest about her struggles will help others feel that they, too, can reach a place of acceptance and forgiveness. When she talks to people trapped in grief, she encourages, "Talk about it, feel it, sit in it, experience it. It's painful and it's scary and it's dark. But when you have support and you go to therapy or a support group or a best friend—I'm telling you, the sooner you can release the pain, the sooner your life can move forward."

The path she chose has allowed Tanya to release her anger and grief and to live more fully in the present. Forgiveness did not come easily—she had to confront her darkest moments in order to release them—but the process allowed her to escape from the trauma inflicted by others and to live the life that she chooses for herself.

As the oldest child in my family, I can't imagine going through what Tanya experienced and being able to for-give. Her story is proof of her strength, self-awareness, and compassion. In talking to Tanya, I was deeply moved by the way she spoke about Nicole—still having love for her sister but not carrying anger toward the man she believes to be responsible for her death. Her journey again showed me that there is no one timetable for the process of forgiveness. We might think that we need to hurry up and forgive in order to move on with our lives, but that doesn't usually end up being as beneficial as we think it might be. It's clear from talking with Tanya that it is really *how* we forgive that dictates our quality of life moving forward. I have certainly forgiven too quickly myself, and was then faced with the need to circle back and work through a situation I had thought I'd moved on from. While the work to get to a place of forgiveness may be some of the most challenging work you will do, the payoff will be immeasurable.

Adel Altamimi

Warrior of Love

"If I am not forgiving them, I am still in a destructive relationship with them."

—*Dr. Henry Cloud*

I n 1998, when Adel Altamimi was nine years old, he made a discovery that would change his life forever. Riding his bike home from school in his hometown of Baghdad, he came upon a dojo, a martial arts studio, filled with rows of men rehearsing karate forms. Adel was a strong child who enjoyed challenging himself, so he was immediately drawn to the crisp, disciplined movements of the men. He soon joined the dojo and dedicated himself to the art of karate. Over the ensuing years, he developed a deep bond with his sensei Moyed, a bond that resembled a father-son relationship. Then, in 2003, the United States invaded Iraq. Adel recalls going to visit his sensei at his house, as he often did. He opened the door to find Moyed's family members distraught and covered in blood.

They told him that Moyed had been killed in a bombing at their local gas station. The bomb had killed four hundred people in the vicinity. This was Adel's initiation into the horrors of war, and into the journey of forgiveness.

In 2004, Adel and his brother decided to channel their anger over Moyed's death to help rebuild Iraq. At this point, Iraqis had to choose between joining the Americans in their fight to forge a democracy or joining al-Qaeda. Adel believed in the American vision, so he, his brother, and his cousins began working alongside the Americans as convoy drivers. Every morning on his way into work, he passed dead bodies along the roads. He kept Moyed in the back of his mind as he adjusted to this new reality. During this time, the terrorist group was on the lookout for Iraqis helping the Americans. One day, Adel's mother saw her son's name on an al-Qaeda list of suspected collaborators. She sent word to Adel, who was in hiding, not to go outside—not even to come home. He understood that he was risking his life when he decided to make his way back to his family. On his way home, he came upon a fake checkpoint. Al-Qaeda insurgents shot into his car, but he made it home unharmed.

In 2005, when Adel's brother was leaving the U.S. Marines base, an al-Qaeda sniper shot him in the head. He was transported by marine helicopter to a military hospital. The surgeons saved his life, but he lost both of his eyes and his nose.

Adel's family wanted him to quit his job, but he was determined to continue. A few months later, Adel, his two friends, and one of his friend's brother were leaving work when they came upon another fake checkpoint. The insurgents questioned them, then ordered them out of the car. When they inspected his car, they found the U.S. Marines badges. They beat Adel and the others. Then they put plastic bags over their heads and threw them in a car to transport them to a secret location. Adel felt sure he would be killed. He thought of his family: his oldest brother, killed by Saddam Hussein; his other brother, blinded and disfigured; his mother, father, and younger brother, waiting for him at home. Adel and his friends were locked in a room and the plastic bags were removed. They were seated in front of a camera. Masked men began yelling at them, calling them terrorists for helping the marines. Their captors told them they were going to kill them for their involvement with the Americans. They grabbed his friend Ahmed and Ahmed's brother, and placed them in front of Adel. Then they began decapitating them while Adel watched in shock. "I was really feeling like, 'I'm going to die—this is my end.'"

The horror was impossible to process. Only moments before, Adel had been hanging out with Ahmed, laughing and joking, and now his lifeless body was propped before him. The terrorists then brought the severed heads over to Adel, taunting him. He remembers becoming emotionless at the sight of the blood. In that moment, the only thing that came to his mind was his mother, father, and his sensei Moyed. He recalled thinking to himself that he would finally be seeing his sensei soon in the afterlife. He remained calm, knowing that soon he would be among loved ones. He began praying to God. As Adel prayed, he heard loud gunshots all around him. U.S. Marines burst into the building. They shouted for him to run up to the top of the building for safety. "'Don't worry—we got you. We got you!' And they cut us free. It was like a dream." Adel and his friend were the only two rescued by the marines that day. Shortly after, Adel returned to work.

Throughout 2006 and 2007, conditions in Iraq deteriorated. Adel and his family moved to Lebanon. Then Adel's father decided that they needed to move to the United States. After enduring such extreme trauma, Adel found arriving in America to be jarring and surreal. He was grateful to be in a safe place, but he felt isolated and guilty for having made it out alive when so many of his friends and family members had not been so lucky. His brother also struggled to adapt, trying to navigate a new world without his vision. He fell into a deep depression and attempted suicide several times. Adel, too, became profoundly depressed, plunged into a dark place—unable to sleep, overwhelmed by stress. Like his brother, Adel attempted suicide. "I was really angry, like really pissed. Anxiety, I can't sleep. I was breaking everything. It's not me." Adel wanted to leave America and return to Iraq to die. He remembers his dad sitting him down and saying, "You're just going to give up? You believe in God, and He saved you. He brought you to this beautiful country. You have to fight. Back to training—back to fighting. That's what you love. Remember Moyed." His father reminded him that his true passion lay in his ability to fight. He told his son to do it in honor of his sensei. This reignited the fire inside Adel.

Adel moved to Los Angeles, where he began training at a gym and working at a restaurant washing dishes. He taught himself English by watching movies and TV shows, and slowly he became more comfortable in his new home. He excelled in the world of mixed martial arts, impressing everyone who saw him train. The journey wasn't easy: he lived out of his car, slept in a gym, and trained day and night to improve his fighting skills. He fell in love and had his heart shattered, but he always managed to pick himself up and fight on. Each day he grew stronger, faster, and more dangerous inside the ring. In 2019, Adel signed as a professional MMA fighter with Bellator, an American mixed martial arts promotion company, and his career has continued to flourish.

When Adel speaks about the hardships that he has endured, he does so with a practicality and confidence that show his ability to rise above the past. The key to his survival—the source of his hope—has been his relationship with God. Every time he felt like giving up, he would talk to God and be reminded of how many obstacles he had overcome and how many blessings he had received along the way. His faith that God guides his destiny gives him the strength to absorb the blows and fight on. Despite all he has suffered and all he has lost—the family and friends who have been killed—Adel holds no bitterness. "I never hate someone. I never hate." And he is committed to sharing his faith with others. "I always want to be someone people look up to and believe in—believe in my life, and believe in God. That's why I always talk about God."

In a sport often blinded by materialism and ego, Adel wants to be a beacon of hope and humility. "I want the new kids to come, too. I don't want to be that person who tries to make money from it. I want to be someone people look up to. This is who I am. I feel like God's with me." The faith that guided him through the war-torn streets of Baghdad, the faith that lifted him after the loss of his sensei, the destruction of his home, and the murder of his closest friends—this is what sustains Adel today. "God is first; he wants me to stay alive," he says. Adel pours his heart into rebuilding, never focusing on revenge; his goal is always to make the world a better place. And in this fight, the greatest weapon is love: "I just love my family, love people around me, love anyone. I just try to help people wherever I can. As a human being, we need love. God is all about love." And love, for Adel, is the essence of forgiveness: "If you read the Bible or the Koran, He talks always about love and forgiveness, and forgive like it doesn't matter that we have been hurt—it doesn't matter what you do. Always, God opens His door for you. If somebody hurts me? I will forgive. This is me in life and in God. It's love." Adel knows that he wouldn't have been able to get through all that he has survived without the presence of God in his life. "Put God in your life and you will be saved. What I went through—because I believe in Him, He saved me. And that's why I love this country, because it saved me, too."

Despite everything that Adel has survived, he knows that tomorrow is never guaranteed. He wants people to know that they should "always show love and forgiveness. Never hate someone." If he ever came in contact with the man who took his brother's sight, he wouldn't seek revenge. If the man asked for forgiveness, he would forgive him. Adel recalls how his father never harbored hate toward anyone. If someone stole from his father, he would tell Adel that it was okay—that person obviously needed the money more than they did. He was raised reading the Koran and being taught the importance of forgiveness. That's why, for Adel, the only way to escape the hatred and violence that consumed his homeland was through forgiveness. Forgiving and loving all has become his life's mission, for which he credits God and His teachings in the Koran.

"Forgiveness is just love. God is all about love, and it's any culture, it's any religion."

Adel may get knocked down, but he always rises again with a full heart, ready to forgive, eager to spread love, committed to overcoming hatred. Few have lost so much and yet had so much to give. Adel's story shows us all that each day is a gift, every hardship is a lesson, and every breath we take should fill us with hope for a brighter tomorrow.

Of all the stories in this book, Adel's was the most difficult for me to hear. The horrors he experienced were unimaginable, and yet he is able to reflect on them with a sense of calm and clarity that is hard to fathom. Like so many of the other people with whom I spoke, he credits his faith with his resiliency. When events transcend our ability to comprehend, a belief in a higher power can keep us strong and help us to restore hope.

When I was talking to Adel about his story, I was stunned by his positivity. Most of us will never experience anything remotely like what he has endured. After interviewing him, I left reconsidering various parts of my life in a new light. Situations I once felt were so challenging and almost impossible to deal with, I now saw as mere speed bumps instead of roadblocks. Sometimes, when we are able to shift our perspective by taking a step back and looking at the bigger picture, it changes the way we might act—and react—moving forward. I wanted to include Adel's story not to minimize the challenges anyone reading this book might face, but rather to exemplify that by shifting our attitude and outlook, we can prevent our past from dictating our future.

Cora Jakes Coleman

Taking Back Power

> "Forgiveness gives me boundaries because it un-
> hooks me from the hurtful person, and then I can
> act responsibly, wisely."
>
> —*Dr. Henry Cloud*

Growing up the daughter of Bishop T. D. Jakes and Serita Jakes, Cora Jakes Coleman was taught about the impor-tance of forgiveness from her earliest days. Over the course of many years and many enduring relationships, Cora has "found that when I walk with a heart of forgiveness, it requires a love that is unconditional for myself." She learned that the love she had for herself would allow her to act with dignity and grace in any situation. By trying to remain humble and kind, living in a space of forgiveness comes naturally and has allowed her to "keep ahold of my power."

Cora's ability to forgive was challenged by someone she thought of as a sister. She had struggled for years to conceive a child, when her friend Julia* decided to allow her to legally adopt her son. Three years later, Julia decided that she wanted to raise the boy as her own. Cora and Julia went to court and fought for the custody of the child. This sense of betrayal—one of her closest confidantes publicly exposing her deepest struggles with infertility and motherhood—was unlike anything she had dealt with before.

The pain of this betrayal was compounded by the loss of a friendship that she'd thought would last forever. As she struggled with the fact that she would have to end her friendship with Julia, she often turned to the Parable of the Tares, from the Bible: "In this parable, a fieldworker plants his field with wheat. While he's resting, an enemy comes in and plants the field with tare [weeds]. So when the man wakes up in the morning, he sees that his entire field has been reseeded. Instead of cutting all the tare out, he decides to let the wheat and the tare grow together. Once they have matured, he makes the decision to uproot the tare and burn the tare and uproot the wheat and make it harvest." Cora related to being the wheat trying hard to keep a good hold on Julia, the tare, but she felt that the Lord was telling her she needed to separate herself. "I could not keep attaching myself to people, to relationships that were never supposed to be planted with me to begin with and that were going to be burned and destroyed at the end of

* This name has been changed to protect her identity.

the day. So I had to make a conscious decision to be fruitful and to be productive and to not be a savior to situations that were never meant for me to save."

Cora and Julia fought for custody of her son for almost two years. It wasn't until the end that Cora really felt that she was able to say she had forgiven Julia. Throughout those two years, Cora prayed for her friend daily. She would try to reach out to her to remind her of the friendship they had and the memories they had made together, with the hope that Julia would realize how hurtful the betrayal was. She recalls praying for her so much that she reached a point where God told her to stop praying—that it was okay to let her friend go. Cora wrote Julia a long letter saying she had forgiven her for everything. She asked for Julia's forgiveness, too. After writing that letter, Cora was finally able to let the friendship go.

It was hard for Cora to accept that a seemingly forever friendship had come to an end. She felt that she needed to forgive herself for becoming attached to something that was not meant to be permanent. She had to detach from that pattern and "walk into my destiny and not feel bad about it."

Looking back, Cora knows that being able to forgive and move on is a responsibility that we owe to ourselves in order to maintain healthy and productive relationships. While her friend is no longer in her life, Cora is at peace with her decision. Having forgiven her friend, she can move forward without resentment or bitterness. Not keeping Julia in her life "doesn't mean that I haven't forgiven her; it means that I have taken my power back, my responsibility back." Cora knows that relationships have their ups and downs, and some friendships can survive the strains. Some friends work through their issues and are able to have what she calls "building-block moments"—when both people in the friendship are able to admit their faults and move forward with a better understanding of each other's needs.

Today, the mention of her old friend's betrayal does not trigger Cora. "It's emotionless to me now. It wasn't always. But that's how I know I have forgiven her. I have forgiven you and so you have no more effect on my emotion." Looking back, she views the end of her friendship more as a disappointment.

Cora began teaching her children about forgiveness at an early age. She instructs them to say, "I apologize," instead of "I'm sorry"—and to learn the difference between the two. For her, "I apologize" is about taking responsibility for your own actions, while "I'm sorry" doesn't adequately acknowledge your role in the wrongdoing or indicate that you intend to change your ways. As she says, "An apology is for you, and that means you're not going to do or respond in that way ever again. That's what an apology means." Whether you are offering or receiving forgiveness, it is an opportunity to release the pain and guilt and move forward renewed.

For Cora, forgiveness is not something you give to another; it's something you give yourself: "Forgiveness isn't about the person who's betraying you or lying to you or denying you; forgiveness, for me, is about me taking my power back and not allowing them to affect me emotionally." We know we have truly forgiven someone who has harmed us, she says, when they no longer have the power to affect us emotionally: "They don't have the power to make you angry or discouraged or insecure about yourself."

Not all friendships last forever. A childhood friendship that's wonderful at age fourteen might no longer be working for you at age twenty-eight—and that's okay. We change and we grow, and sometimes friendships can't change and grow as our needs do. It can be painful, but there are times when you have to examine an old friendship and ask yourself if it's still healthy for you as you mature. In the past, when I felt this doubt, I would often push the feelings away, because ending an old friendship seemed wrong. Over the years, I've learned that, sometimes, ending a relationship is the only way to stay true to yourself.

When Cora talked about the feeling of needing to separate herself from her friend for her own well-being, I could relate. Sometimes, no matter how hard we try to help the other person or make the friendship work, it is healthier for us to move on instead. When Cora told me that she ended her friendship through a letter saying she forgave her friend, I was reminded that I had done something similar when I ended my friendship with my best friend of twenty-five years. And in my experience, I agree with Cora that you know you have truly forgiven someone when you hear their name and you have no reaction to it anymore. For me, it took several years to get to that place—it's different for everyone. However long the process takes—from friendship to betrayal and finally to forgiveness—the journey is one of reclaiming your power as a way forward.

I loved that Cora referred to the journey of forgiveness as a "building-block moment"—I couldn't agree with her more. While those moments for me were incredibly challenging and painful, I look back on them now as times that made me stronger. I always try to look for the lesson in everything, and, for me, the betrayal of a close friend is an opportunity to do just that: grieve the loss, forgive, and move on in order to live a full and free life.

Sebastián Marroquín

Owning the Sins of My Father

> "Forgiveness is above all a personal choice, a deci-
> sion of the heart to go against the natural instinct
> to pay back evil with evil."
>
> —*Pope John Paul II*

S ebastián Marroquín was born in Medellín, Colombia, in
1977. His earliest memories of his father are typical:
learning how to swim, playing board games together, decorat-
ing the Christmas tree. His father was always loving and attentive, expressing his feelings freely, wanting only the best for his
son. But as Sebastián grew older, he began to realize that his
father's life was far from normal. The family lived on a large
compound. There were no telephones. They rarely traveled,
and when they did, they were surrounded by bodyguards.
Then his father began to appear on the news, sometimes for
his public projects—funding the construction of a school or
soccer stadium—and sometimes for his less altruistic projects.

Sebastián's father was the notorious Colombian drug lord Pablo Escobar.

As Sebastián grew older, he became increasingly aware of the violent empire his father had built—and the many people who were killed in order to sustain it. He voiced his disapproval, telling his father, "I love you, but I don't believe in what you are doing. I think you are causing a lot of harm to a lot of people. You should find a way to leave everything behind and find peace for yourself and for the family you have." For Escobar, there was no turning back. This left Sebastián in a torn reality, drawn toward the gentle father he loved but alienated from the brutal drug trafficker who was terrorizing the nation. He explained to his father that he had no intention to follow in his footsteps; if his father used violence to prove his points, Sebastián would use his heart and words to build a very different world.

In 1993, Escobar's reign of terror ended when he was shot down in a gunfight with the Colombian police. That's the official story. Sebastián is sure that his father ended his own life. Escobar had promised his family—as well as his enemies—that he would never be captured alive; he himself would be the one responsible for the bullet in his head. On the day of his death, Escobar used the phone ten times to contact his family. Sebastián had been raised to never use the phone; the police could trace the calls too easily. His family was being closely monitored by police after their attempts to flee the country had failed. Escobar used those calls to let his family know that he loved them. It is clear to Sebastián that his father ended his own life to protect the lives of those he loved the most. "He knew in his heart that if he didn't appear dead, the next ones would be his own family. His wife and sons." When asked if he has any anger toward his father for taking his own life, Sebastián says, "I see that my father's suicide was perhaps his biggest act of love for his family. He knew that the only way to set us free was to kill himself."

But his father's death didn't end the legacy of violence.

When Sebastián learned of his father's death, he was overcome with rage. He swore to a journalist—on live radio—that he was going to kill the men who had killed his father. Only ten minutes later, he knew he had made a terrible mistake. He immediately apologized to the Colombian people, declaring, "If one day I can do what it takes to bring peace to this country, I will do it." He then sent a message to all the men employed by his father, asking them to end their violence and refrain from harming anyone else. Despite this, his father's rivals put a $4 million bounty on his head. For Sebastián, this was a time of constant fear; he couldn't trust anyone, not even the police. He and his family fled Colombia—first to Mozambique, and then to Argentina. It was then that the loyal son who had been named Juan Escobar after his father had to change his name.

To escape his father's legacy, Sebastián decided to assume

responsibility for his father's crimes—crimes he had no part in—and appeal to the victims for forgiveness. He documented this process in a film called *Sins of My Father*. This project allowed him the opportunity to approach the families of his father's victims and to ask for their forgiveness on behalf of his father. "I really believe that I have to take some kind of responsibility for my father's actions. Even if I didn't commit any crime, I felt responsible for asking for their forgiveness." His friends told him he was crazy to embark on this mission of forgiveness, saying his father's victims would never forgive him—he would just be opening old wounds and subjecting himself to their revenge. But Sebastián needed to try.

He first approached the families of two of his father's most prominent victims: the political leaders Rodrigo Lara and Luis Carlos Galán. As Colombia's minister of justice, Lara was determined to expose Escobar and the Medellín Cartel. He was gunned down in 1984 by one of Escobar's assassins. Galán, a popular presidential candidate and outspoken critic of the drug cartels, was shot dead at a campaign rally in 1989. Both families welcomed Sebastián with open arms and open hearts. His willingness to assume responsibility for his father's actions, and the families' willingness to forgive, marked a turning point in the culture of retribution that had dominated Colombia for decades.

Sebastián next reached out to the victims of Avianca Flight 203. The commercial plane crashed in November 1989 after a bomb detonated on board, killing all 107 crew and passengers. Escobar had planned the bombing in the attempt to assassinate another presidential candidate hostile to his cartel. Again, the families accepted Sebastián's plea for forgiveness. I asked him what he would do if someone told him that they wouldn't forgive him for his father's actions. He said that he would respect their decision: "When you ask for forgiveness, you shouldn't expect answers." He believes that people have accepted his plea for forgiveness because they know that he is coming from a place of love, and not politics.

In 2009, Sebastián spoke publicly about forgiveness for the first time. Many Colombians were surprised, as forgiveness and reconciliation were not commonly discussed in the country. For decades, the mentality was "Shoot the guy and that's it, game over—that's how we solve things in Colombia." But today, when Sebastián walks the streets of Colombia, strangers often stop to thank him for the work he is doing. The positive effect it has had on the nation has been huge. For him, the documentary about his father was just the beginning of a conversation—between victims and their attackers—that continues today and promises to lift both groups from the trauma of the past and restore a path to reconciliation. Sebastián truly believes that peace is possible, even in Colombia.

When Sebastián embarked on this journey, it was not only important to him to ask for forgiveness on behalf of his father; it was also important to him because he hoped one day to have a son. Sebastián knew what it was like to deal with the hate directed at him because of his father's crimes, and he didn't want to pass this legacy on to his son. "For the future of my son, I have to do everything that is necessary to leave him at least a better world." He waited more than twenty years to have a child because he and his wife wanted to make sure they wouldn't be pursued by the victims of his father's crimes. He says, "My son is a guarantee that I'm going to behave for the rest of my life." Sebastián wants to be honest with his now six-year-old son about who his grandfather was and the crimes he committed. But he also wants to share with his son how loving his grandfather was with his family. He knows that if his father were alive, he would give his grandson the same unconditional love that he'd showered upon Sebastián. He wants his son to know the real Pablo Escobar, and not just the gruesome caricature so often portrayed in the media. This is what fuels Sebastián's passion for recording his father's life in books and films. He wants to leave his son a positive legacy—a legacy based on truth that inspires him to follow a path of love and forgiveness. He says that he prays every day that his son "won't ever dare to be like his own grandfather."

I asked Sebastián if he forgives his father for the crimes he committed and for leaving his son with such a terrible legacy. He responded that he never felt that he had to forgive his father: "I'm not God, so I don't have the power to judge him.

Second, being part of him—that doesn't give me neutral perspective about things, because I'm very close to him. To be honest, my father only gave me love. I only received love from him. So how can I hate, or how can I put myself in a position to say, 'I will forgive you for this or for that' or 'I condemn you for that or this'? I really don't think that's the way a son should behave. I never think about the possibility of judging my own father. I think that's God's job, and it is society's job."

Sebastián still travels throughout Colombia, making amends with families affected by his father's violence. He has seen the positive effect this journey has had on the families he has met. "After the forgiveness process, of course, they felt better. They felt that they could renounce, in a way, all the hate and the pain. I think that forgiveness is not about forgetting things. Perhaps it's about feeling. It's not about telling someone, 'You need to forget something.' It's about healing. It's about abandoning the hate that makes us feel sick."

Today, Sebastián is an architect, the author of two books, and a two-time documentary filmmaker. But he knows that part of his identity will always be that he is the son of Pablo Escobar. He knows that his journey of forgiveness will never end. This is his life's mission. He has had the chance to become friends with the families of his father's victims, and this gives Sebastián hope. Whenever he goes back to Colombia, he visits with these families and they welcome him into their homes and into their hearts. "That leaves me a lot of hope. This cannot change the past, but I'm changing the present, and that of course will affect the future."

I reached out to Sebastián after seeing his documentary and reading about the great work he was doing. I knew that a man who dedicated his life to asking for forgiveness on behalf of his father must be a man who understood the process intimately, who knew the remarkable healing power of making amends. What surprised me was how deep Sebastián's love for his father had been and how profoundly the act of forgiveness had transformed his life and the lives of countless Colombians.

Sebastián's decision to travel the world seeking forgiveness from complete strangers, yet never knowing the response he might get, showed me how forgiveness is not really about two parties coming to a conclusion to forgive. Instead, what's important is the very act of expressing forgiveness. Whether we ask for forgiveness or give forgiveness, we are often afraid of the response we might get. Sebastián's journey showed me that the act of requesting forgiveness is never easy—even when you are doing it on someone else's behalf—but the gesture of doing so is what makes all the difference. And that can leave you feeling lighter moving forward.

Sebastián's public appeal for forgiveness has helped transform one of the darkest chapters in Colombia's history into a story of hope. It taught me that forgiveness is a power that transcends generations and can heal rifts that once tore a whole country apart.

Conclusion

I'm a different person today because of the stories in this book, and now that you've read it, perhaps you are, too. When I started this journey, I honestly didn't know what to expect. Once I started, I knew I would be forever changed by the stories I was told, and I was told a lot of stories. In fact, I heard so many that I couldn't possibly include all of them in this book, because they came to me, and at me, in almost every conversation I've had in the past few years.

When people would ask me what I was working on, I would tell them, "I'm working on a book on forgiveness." I would tell them about the people I was interviewing, and about my own journey with forgiveness. Immediately, people's faces would change. Some smiled, some paused, others instantly wept. Almost without warning, stories of forgiveness would come tumbling out. Stories about heartbreaking ruptures in families, fights with siblings, breaks in partnerships and marriages. Others involved ongoing struggles to forgive, while still others involved insistence, amid tears, that they would never forgive. All told stories of deeply personal journeys to forgiveness and freedom. But the one thing they all had in common? They wanted to know more.

Whether we've received it or given it, or whether we're still struggling with it—none of us is a stranger to forgiveness. What stuck with me most during this journey is how deeply curious everyone seems to be about understanding forgiveness—about finding a way to practice it in their own lives, whether it's with a friend, a spouse or former spouse, a family member, or a deceased parent. During this process, I was struck by how the people I interviewed had found a way to take their pain and turn it into purpose. Their strength astounds me.

WHILE WRITING THIS BOOK, there were days after an interview when I could barely speak, days when I couldn't think about anything but the stories I was hearing and the incredible strength each of these people displayed. I cried with some of them and I was inspired by all of them.

"Forgiveness" is one of those words that stop people in their tracks. It carries a certain weight. It forces us to ask ourselves uncomfortable questions: Can I forgive a hurt I should have never experienced? Can I forgive someone who never said, "I'm sorry"? If I'm still angry, does that mean I haven't forgiven? And is it all right if I never get to a place where I can say, "I forgive you"? I know now that the search for understanding and practicing forgiveness is everywhere. For some, it's easier practiced than for others; I myself have continued to struggle with forgiveness. There have been times in my life when I rejected forgiveness altogether, and there have been times when my ability to call on it surprised me. There were times while writing this book when my past crept up on me; people I thought I had forgiven resurfaced in my life to show me that I actually had more work to do. The knowledge I gained while writing this book helped me shift my perspective on situations I thought I never could. I have found myself going back to these stories to pull me through. Knowing that there are so many ways to practice forgiveness has encouraged me to keep pushing forward with hope and positivity.

We all know what it's like to feel hurt and pain. We've all experienced traumas that disrupted our lives and left us grasping for a restored sense of ourselves. Whether being betrayed by a best friend or spouse, losing a loved one to an act of violence, or surviving a terrible ordeal, we've all lived through events that have changed the course of our lives and presented us with the opportunity to forgive. I use the word "opportunity" because the act of forgiveness is both a gift you give yourself and one you can offer to another person. How you forgive, when you forgive, and whether you forgive at all are choices that will help shape the rest of your life. If you take nothing else from this book, I hope you will realize that forgiveness is not one-size-fits-all. Rather, it takes all shapes and forms, and will likely look different for each of us. It may take a day or a year, or the rest of your life to achieve. Or it may never happen at all. And that's okay.

Forgiveness is rarely a simple act; it's more often an ongoing process to achieve your freedom and peace of mind from a particular incident or person. It is when you no longer carry the resentment, anger, shame, or negative feelings—when you can let them go. It is when you no longer allow an incident to have control over your life—mentally, physically, and spiritually. It is acknowledging the hurt and pain, allowing yourself to feel it, and then getting to a place where you can release it, but not forget it.

My belief is that it is all in God's time, and truthfully, it wasn't until I asked for God's help that I felt I could move forward in my own life. Do I still have times when past wounds might burn a little? Of course. But it's how I shift myself back into perspective—using the tools I've learned from those interviewed in this book—that allows me to live my life free of staying in that old wound. We often find comfort in our anger and pain, and the idea of releasing that can be scary and extremely uncomfortable—at times it can almost feel like a betrayal of your own hurt. Some use their anger from a particular incident to fuel their passion for change, while others hold on to their pain like a possession or a part of their body they can't imagine living without. Each day is an opportunity to try again, if we choose to take it.

As I said in my introduction, I am not an expert on forgiveness, and I doubt I could have done as good a job as many of the people in this book, had I been in their position. Hearing their stories has moved me and inspired me immensely, and it is a blessing to be able to look at forgiveness in a different light. It has reassured me that no matter what comes up in my life in the future, I can consciously choose to forgive. Today, when I experience feelings of anger, sadness, or hurt from an old wound, I consider the incident, acknowledge that I have forgiven, but I am gentle with myself. I remember that I am doing my best and that every day I am given the opportunity to put things into perspective again. When I fall off the path of forgiveness—which we all do—I now know that I have the strength and the tools to reengage no matter how many times it takes me to get to where I want to go. I believe in forgiving, but not forgetting. I believe that each incident in my life has happened for a specific reason, and sometimes we must be patient to realize what that reason is.

I am deeply grateful I embarked on this journey many years ago because it enabled me to not only look harder at my friendships, but at every aspect of my life. The work I've gone through with forgiveness has enabled me to find a more compassionate and empathetic self, and I truly believe that, had I not embarked on this journey, I would not be where I am today, feeling happy, whole, secure, confident, capable, and grateful. So you never know when you take that first step what might happen farther down the road.

If you've picked up this book, you might have the same curiosity about forgiveness that I had. My hope is that this book will help you the same way it has helped me. I am deeply grateful to all the people who shared their courageous and challenging journeys with me—all of them chose to participate because they hoped their stories might help others in similar situations. They all know firsthand how challenging the process of forgiveness truly is—that's why they learned to never judge anyone's experience. It is a lesson I also took away.

My hope is that this book will have the same effect on you as it did me. Most importantly, I hope you realize that you are not alone on your journey with forgiveness and that, however you choose to get there, healing, hope, and love await you on the other side. There is no timetable, so take your time. Try not to judge yourself, or others, and know that at the end of the road, there is a gift waiting for you—the gift of forgiveness.

Now It's Your Turn

Throughout the process of writing this book, I was constantly forced to face my past and my present head-on. People I thought I had forgiven, I actually had not. People I didn't even know I needed to forgive resurfaced, as did situations that I thought I had worked my way through, and I realized that I still had more work to do. There is no way to pass through life without being hurt or hurting others. When these injuries happen, it's up to us to confront them—to understand them, and let them go. It's up to us to *forgive*—to set ourselves free from the burdens of our pasts.

I have found that when we say the word "forgiveness," our minds often return to a person, a place, a situation—something unresolved, something we can't forget. If I have learned one thing from writing this book, it is that forgiveness is deep, challenging, complex, and unique to everyone, but when it is done—truly and completely—forgiveness is the greatest gift you can give to others and to yourself. When we are able to forgive, our lives change for the better, and we are set free.

Now that you have read this book, I encourage you to pause and reflect. Use the space below to write to someone you want to forgive—even if it's yourself—or someone you wish would forgive you. You can keep this note (or notes) to yourself, or you can share it. You can pass this book on to someone you feel might benefit from reading it, and you can tell them about your own journey. Sharing your story and your struggles can help others in theirs—and it can also help you. So write a note to an old friend, a loved one, someone who may not even be on this earth, or to yourself. Write to someone who hurt you or to someone you hurt. And get ready to live a freer and lighter life. Good luck!

_____

_____

_____

_____

_____

_____

Acknowledgments

I would like to first thank every single person in this book for trusting me with their forgiveness journey. Their stories are raw, vulnerable, emotional, and real, and I am beyond grateful that they shared them with me. This book would not have been possible without the love and support of my amazing team: Nena Madonia Oshman and Jan Miller Rich, who have worked with me on all of my books. They provide me with so much love and guidance, and their friendship means the world to me. I am grateful to my editors, Pam Dorman and Jeramie Orton, who have worked on every detail of this book with me and have been incredibly patient and kind. Thank you also to my manager and dear friend Hilary Williams Dunlap, who supports me and fights for all I do and care about every day. I am thankful for Nayon Cho, who patiently and kindly went back and forth many times with me to get this cover perfect. I'm so grateful to my close friends, my amazing family: my mom, who advised me and was an incredible sounding board every step of the way; my sister, Christina, who had the brilliant idea of adding a self-reflection section to this book; my brothers, Patrick and Christopher, and my dad, all of whom supported my writing process and book idea; and my incredibly supportive husband, Chris, who listened, loved, and offered advice as I navigated my way through this book. And to my stepson, Jack, who keeps me laughing always. All of them have listened to each interview, dealt with realizations and struggles I have had, and stood by me as I have gained a better understanding of forgiveness. I am also deeply grateful to Will Thach. I've known Will since I was a kid, and he helped me immensely by pushing me in my writing, my thoughts, and listened to me after each of these interviews and helped me make sense of them.

And finally to all the brave people who gave me their time, who shared with me their wisdom, their pain, their heartbreak, and their hope. This book exists because of you. Thank you.

For more information on forgiveness, look into these organizations doing amazing work in the space:

The Forgiveness Project
Worldwide Forgiveness Alliance

A number of those interviewed here have written their own books. I've listed them below, in case you are interested in finding out more about their stories:

ELIZABETH SMART
My Story (with Chris Stewart)
Where There's Hope: Healing, Moving Forward, and
    Never Giving Up

CHRIS WILLIAMS
Let It Go: A True Story of Tragedy and Forgiveness

IMMACULÉE ILIBAGIZA
Left to Tell: Discovering God Amidst the Rwandan
    Holocaust
Led by Faith: Rising from the Ashes of the Rwandan
    Genocide (Left to Tell)
Our Lady of Kibeho: Mary Speaks to the World from the
    Heart of Africa
Sowing the Seeds of Forgiveness: Sharing Messages of
    Love and Hope After the Rwandan Genocide
A Visit from Heaven
The Boy Who Met Jesus: Segatashya of Kibeho
The Rosary: The Prayer That Saved My Life
The Story of Jesus and Mary in Kibeho: A Prophecy
    Fulfilled

RON HALL

*Same Kind of Different As Me: A Modern-Day Slave, an
International Art Dealer, and the Unlikely Woman
Who Bound Them Together* (with Denver Moore and
Lynn Vincent)

*What Difference Do It Make?: Stories of Hope and
Healing*

*Workin' Our Way Home: The Incredible True Story of a
Homeless Ex-Con and a Grieving Millionaire Thrown
Together to Save Each Other*

DEBORAH COPAKEN

Shutterbabe: Adventures in Love and War

Between Here and April

*Hell Is Other Parents: And Other Tales of Maternal
Combustion*

The Red Book

The ABCs of Adulthood: An Alphabet of Life Lessons

The ABCs of Parenthood: An Alphabet of Parenting Advice

NADIA BOLZ-WEBER

*Salvation on the Small Screen? 24 Hours of Christian
Television*

Pastrix: The Cranky, Beautiful Faith of a Sinner & Saint

Accidental Saints: Finding God in All the Wrong People

Shameless: A Sexual Reformation

Lewis Howes

The School of Greatness: A Real-World Guide to Living Bigger, Loving Deeper, and Leaving a Legacy

The Mask of Masculinity: How Men Can Embrace Vulnerability, Create Strong Relationships, and Live Their Fullest Lives

Scarlett Lewis

Nurturing Healing Love: A Mother's Journey of Hope & Forgiveness

DeVon Franklin

The Wait: A Powerful Practice for Finding the Love of Your Life and the Life You Love (with Meagan Good and Tim Vandehey)

Produced by Faith: Enjoy Real Success without Losing Your True Self (with Tim Vandehey)

The Truth About Men: What Men and Women Need to Know

The Success Commandments: Master the Ten Spiritual Principles to Achieve Your Destiny (with Tim Vandehey)

Michelle LeClair

Perfectly Clear: Escaping Scientology and Fighting for the Woman I Love (with Robin Gaby Fisher)

Sue Klebold
*A Mother's Reckoning: Living in the Aftermath of
    Tragedy* (with an Introduction by Andrew Solomon)

Mark Kelly
Mousetronaut: Based on a (Partially) True Story
Gabby: A Story of Courage and Hope (with Gabrielle
    Giffords)
Astrotwins: Project Rescue
*Enough: Our Fight to Keep America Safe from Gun
    Violence* (with Gabrielle Giffords)

Tanya Brown
*Finding Peace Amid the Chaos: My Escape from
    Depression and Suicide* (with William Croyle)

Cora Jakes Coleman
Faithing It: Bringing Purpose Back to Your Life!
Ferocious Warrior: Dismantle Your Enemy and Rise
*Victory: Having the Edge for Success in the Battlegrounds
    of Life* (with T. D. Jakes)

Sebastián Marroquín
Pablo Escobar: My Father

P.O. 0005407462 202